FAIL
FAST,
FAIL
OFTEN

JEREMY P. TARCHER/PENGUIN

a member of Penguin Group (USA)

New York

FAIL FAST, FAIL OFTEN

How Losing Can Help You Win

Ryan Babineaux, Ph.D.

John Krumboltz, Ph.D.

JEREMY P. TARCHER/PENGUIN
Published by the Penguin Group
Penguin Group (USA) LLC
375 Hudson Street,
New York, New York 10014

USA · Canada · UK · Ireland · Australia
New Zealand · India · South Africa · China

penguin.com
A Penguin Random House Company

Most Tarcher/Penguin books are available at special quantity discounts for bulk purchase
for sales promotions, premiums, fund-raising, and educational needs. Special
books or book excerpts also can be created to fit specific needs. For details, write:
Special.Markets@us.penguingroup.com.

Library of Congress Cataloging-in-Publication Data

Babineaux, Ryan.
    Fail fast, fail often : how losing can help you win / Ryan Babineaux, Ph.D., John Krumboltz, Ph.D.
        p.   cm.
    Includes bibliographical references.
    ISBN 978-0-399-16625-9
    1. Failure (Psychology)   2. Change (Psychology)   3. Career changes.   4. Self-actualization
(Psychology)   5. Success.   I. Krumboltz, John D.   II. Title.
    BF575.F14B33   2013   2013036563
    650.1—dc23

Printed in the United States of America
10   9   8   7   6   5   4   3   2

Book design by Ellen Cipriano

CONTENTS

FAIL
FAST,
FAIL
OFTEN

Preface

THE POINT OF this book is to help you take action in your life. You might think of it as "Action 101" because we teach the basics of getting going and making things happen, even though you may feel apprehensive, unprepared, or afraid of failure.

The ideas presented here arose out of our work as career counselors and educators. In talking to thousands of individuals about their work, we made an important discovery: People who are happy and successful spend less time planning and more time acting. They get out into the world and try new things, make mistakes, and in doing so, benefit from unexpected experiences and opportunities.

Over the years we have developed simple yet powerful techniques to help people take positive action in their lives. These techniques have proven to be effective in our work with a wide range of clients as well as with participants in workshops and university courses. We have helped people accomplish many things—start businesses, write novels, form research foundations, get married, lose a hundred pounds. We do so not by requiring them to make dramatic changes to who they are, but by encouraging them to make small changes to what they *do*.

In the following pages you will find advice on how to follow your interests and take action, even though you may be unsure of your career plans, feel stuck in a rut, or be apprehensive of failure. We provide practical advice on how to trust your enthusiasm and allow it to guide you, break free from habitual behaviors and initiate new adventures, act boldly with minimal preparation, and leverage your strengths for rapid change. Each chapter includes a discussion of cutting-edge research, inspiring stories from the lives of famous and ordinary people alike, and specific steps to put ideas into practice to enact immediate change in your life.

The Happiness Tipping Point

There is more hunger for love and appreciation in
this world than for bread.

—MOTHER TERESA, WINNER OF THE NOBEL PEACE PRIZE

Why we play as children is not because it is our work or because it is
how we learn, though both statements are true; we play because
we are wired for joy, it is imperative as human beings.

—JOHN THORN, BASEBALL HISTORIAN AND AUTHOR OF
BASEBALL IN THE GARDEN OF EDEN: THE SECRET
HISTORY OF THE EARLY GAME

Find a place inside where there's joy, and the
joy will burn out the pain.

—JOSEPH CAMPBELL, AMERICAN MYTHOLOGIST,
WRITER, AND LECTURER

AS COUNSELORS, we often talk to people who are dissatisfied and
seeking change. Some people want to establish a career that makes
them feel more enthusiastic and engaged. Some have creative projects that they wish to pursue—writing a children's book, starting a
leadership workshop, getting their sculptures into a gallery. Some

people want to break free from limiting behaviors—watching TV, eating fast food, getting caught up in codependent relationships—and adopt a more adventurous and spontaneous approach to life. Then there are those who don't have a clear idea of what they want but just feel the need to strike out in new directions and have fresh experiences.

When people are unhappy they tend to fixate on what they feel is wrong with their lives. They think that if they can quit their dead-end job, break off their relationship with their selfish girlfriend or boyfriend, move to a more exciting city, find supportive friends, overcome their bad habits, have a child (or have their current children leave for college), erase their self-doubts, or discover their true calling, *then* they will be ready to let loose and have fun. You might call this the "not yet" view of life, as it is based on the assumption that you can't enjoy yourself until you escape your current problems. This view has been encouraged by a legion of therapists and counselors who say that you must overcome your emotional hang-ups and negative thinking before you will be ready for major change.

Below is a list of some common ways we have heard the "not yet" view of life expressed. Do any of these sound familiar to you?

I will be ready to get going when:
- The economy picks up
- I feel inspired
- Someone tells me the right thing to do
- I have more money in savings
- The kids leave for college
- Things settle down
- I am in a more supportive relationship
- I discover my inner child
- I quit my dead-end job

- I feel more confident
- I forgive and am forgiven
- I finish my project
- My house is cleaned up
- I come up with a plan
- I overcome my limiting beliefs
- I do my taxes
- I am absolutely certain
- I attend a few more workshops
- I get permission
- I am better prepared
- I don't feel so tired

Focus on Opportunities, Not Problems

The "not yet" view is not only wrong, it presents a surefire way to block you from the beneficial effects of happenstance. When you focus on the shortcomings in your life, drag your feet, and belabor your bad habits and neuroses, you see nothing but your own misery. You become blind to opportunities and don't take actions that lead to change. The "not yet" view also makes change costly and unpleasant. If you think that you need to fix all your problems before you can have fun and try new things, then the preparation becomes so daunting that you don't even want to get started.

We have found that the best way to empower people to transform their lives is not by helping them to resolve their problems, but by encouraging them to pursue what they enjoy. No matter what your circumstances, there are always fun things you can do—there are inspiring people you can meet, curiosities you can pursue, unknown places you can visit, wonders of the world you can

What Does Your Fun-Meter Say?

Suppose that one day you find out that your great-uncle Elmore has just died. You hardly knew your uncle, but from what you have heard from your family, he was a peculiar fellow. The handful of encounters you had with him were as a child, when you experienced his unpleasant habit of saying hello by pulling on your ear and saying "Shazam!" So you are somewhat surprised to receive a letter from your great-uncle's estate attorney requesting that you attend the reading of the will.

You arrive at a stuffy legal office with a room filled with strangers. As the reading of the will begins, you are surprised to find that your great-uncle Elmore was quite wealthy. You are even more shocked to hear that you have been left $100 million, albeit with some peculiar stipulations.

Your great-uncle was a crazy inventor, and his proudest accomplishment was the creation of a wrist-worn gadget he called the fun-meter. It records a measure of the degree of enjoyment you are experiencing—how enthusiastic, vital, curious, and appreciative you are feeling. It rates enjoyment on a scale of one to ten, with one being down-in-the-dumps and ten being happy-as-can-be. The stipulations of your uncle's will are the following: You are to wear the fun-meter at all times. Each day the fun-meter will take the highest enjoyment reading for the day and wirelessly transmit it to the estate attorney's office. If the reading never falls below a value of seven over the course of the next year, then you will receive the $100 million. But if on any day the high for the day falls below seven, then you will receive nothing.

Let's say you decide to take on the challenge of wearing the fun-meter. Right away you are going to have to live life like it really matters. You can't let a single day pass without finding time to have at least a few moments of unadulterated joy. So here's the question: What action would you take on the first day?

appreciate. No matter how trapped you may feel in your current life, there are positive actions you can take and new experiences to be had.

If you are feeling unsettled and uncertain about your life and career, you may be a little suspicious of the idea that you should spend more time enjoying yourself. After all, isn't establishing a career supposed to be deadly serious business? (Our response: a resounding no!) When you are stressed out and unhappy, you may not feel very enthusiastic about finding ways to bring more joy into your life. You may prefer to wait until you have a better handle on your situation before you take on anything new. But sticking with your current way of doing things is the way to ensure that things stay exactly as they are. It is quite simple: If you want your life to change, you have to take different actions.

Passionate Action Is Smart Action

Successful people make a habit of pursuing what they enjoy. They take actions that are aligned with their passions and avoid things that dampen their engagement in life. They do so not just because it makes them happier, but because it makes them smarter. By doing what you love, you place yourself in an appreciative, opportunity-focused mind-set that allows you to think more creatively, work more productively, and capitalize on unexpected opportunities. You don't have to take our word for it. There is a growing body of research that shows how a sense of enjoyment makes people more productive, sociable, and innovative.

In a series of research experiments spanning two decades, psychologist Alice Isen at Cornell University has shown that people who experience positive feelings think differently. In one study, the researchers tested the clinical reasoning of physicians.[1] They placed some of the doctors in a positive mood by giving them a bag of candy before diagnosing a case of a patient with liver disease. Physicians with a positive mood more quickly integrated case information. They were also less likely to get stuck pursuing initial thoughts that would end in a premature diagnosis. In another study, Isen found that negotiators who were feeling good were more likely to discover integrative and flexible solutions in a complex bargaining task. Taken together, Isen and her colleagues' years of research show that people who feel good are more adaptive in their thinking and better able to process complex information.

Over the last thirty years, Harvard University researcher Teresa Amabile and her colleagues have explored what leads people to be happy and creative at work. Amabile has found that people are most creative when they are engaged in work that is intrinsically motivating—when the work itself is a source of joy, satisfaction, and interest. In contrast, decreased creativity is associated with work that is done for a good salary, prestige, or some other external reward. In one experiment, seventy-two creative writers were asked to write a short poem on the topic of snow.[2] The participants were then broken into different groups and asked to complete a "Reasons for Writing" questionnaire, which asked them to rank seven reasons for being a writer. For one group, the reasons listed were all extrinsic, such as "You have heard of cases where one best-selling novel or collection of poems has made the author financially secure." Another group completed a questionnaire with reasons for writing that were intrinsic, such as "You enjoy the opportunity for self-expression." The third group completed a neutral task of reading a short story.

In the second phase of the experiment, the three groups were asked to write a short poem on the subject of laughter. After the seventy-two writers had finished, a group of twelve writers was

Tulsa City-County Library

Martin Regional Library

To Renew: www.tulsalibrary.org

918-549-7323

Date: 9/17/2022

Time: 4:58:20 PM

Fines/Fees Owed: $0.00

Total Checked Out This Session: 2

Checked Out

Title: Let them see you : the guide for leveragin
your diversity at work / Porter Braswell with Rya
Gallo
Barcode: 32345088967832
Due Date: 10-01-22

Title: Fail fast, fail often : how losing can help y
win / Ryan Babineaux, Ph.D., John Krumboltz,
Ph.D.
Barcode: 32345073705015
Due Date: 10-01-22

Thank you for visiting the library!

asked to judge independently the creativity of all the poems. The poems written before completing the questionnaire showed no difference in quality. But the poems written by writers who completed questionnaires with intrinsic-focused questions were significantly more creative than those by writers who considered extrinsic factors. In other words, just thinking for a few minutes about writing for external rewards reduced the creative performance of people who loved to write. These results provide a telling example of how sacrificing personal joy for external rewards can produce a significant drop in the inventiveness of one's work.

In another research project, Amabile and her colleagues studied 12,000 aggregate days of employee diaries from 238 people.[3] In their diaries, participants were asked to provide concrete details of tasks completed, who was involved, and how they felt about their work. Amabile found that there was a 50 percent increase in the odds of a person having a valuable creative idea on a day when he or she was feeling positive. Positive mood also led to a carryover effect: The more positive a person's mood on a given day, the more likely he or she was to have a creative idea on the next day or even the day after. In other words, the joy that you experience on one day can lead to ideas and insights that pop up much later.

Psychologist Barbara Fredrickson at the University of North Carolina at Chapel Hill has theorized that positive emotions tend to broaden the range of people's thoughts and actions, while negative emotions have a constraining effect. In a research study with 104 college students, Fredrickson and her colleagues had participants watch film clips to induce a positive, negative, or neutral mood.[4] Participants were then asked to perform a task where they determined which of two images was similar to a standard image. Participants who experienced negative emotions focused narrowly on local details of the images, while those who experienced positive emotions attended more to global features. This suggests that positive emotions lead to a broader, more comprehensive method of thinking. These results, as well as those from a number of other studies, led Fredrickson to conclude that positive emotions encourage novel and varied thoughts and actions. Negative emotions, in contrast, result in narrow, survival-oriented thinking and behaviors.

In her Broaden-and-Build theory of positive emotions, Fredrickson suggests that when you are feeling good, it encourages you to think more flexibly and engage in playful, exploratory actions.[5] These actions can then expose you to opportunities that help you build enduring personal resources and relationships. Thus, even though the experience of joy may be temporary, it can lead to actions that create a lasting impact on your life.

Fredrickson's insights have been born out in our own experience. In studying the lives of thousands of people, we have seen time and time again that important opportunities and insights often arise as a result of pursuing one's passion. John's life provides a wonderful example of this. He grew up in a midwestern town, where he enjoyed playing a variety of competitive sports. One of his favorites was tennis, which he taught himself in middle school and continued to play on his high school team. When he went to college, John joined the tennis team, which held competitive matches with other colleges. On the long car rides to matches, he got to know the tennis coach, Dr. Wallar.

During his sophomore year, John received a letter asking him to declare his major. Having no idea what to choose, he tossed out the letter. A month later another letter arrived asking him to declare his major, which he similarly disposed of. Finally, he received a third letter, which stated that if he did not report to the Registrar's Office to declare a major by 5 p.m. on the following Friday, his registration would be terminated.

At this point John did not know what to do. He had never received advice on how to go about choosing a major, so he thought it would be best to seek help. The only person he could think of talking to was his tennis coach, Dr. Wallar, so he made an appointment to see him at 4 p.m. on Friday. When John saw Dr. Wallar, he wasted no time beating around the bush. "Dr. Wallar," he said hurriedly, "within the next hour I have to declare a major or my registration will be terminated. What do you think I should major in?"

Now, it turns out that Dr. Wallar was not only the tennis coach but also the college's sole faculty member in psychology. So it is perhaps unsurprising that without missing a beat, Dr. Wallar replied, "Psychology, of course."

"OK, thanks," John called out over his shoulder as he dashed out the door. He rushed to the registrar, grabbed the appropriate form, wrote "psychology" on the line for declaring a major, and signed his name. With great relief he walked away with thirty minutes to spare.

John went on to great success as a psychologist. He is a distinguished faculty member at a top university, has authored well-received books, won numerous awards, is a keynote speaker at conferences around the world, and has been designated a Living Legend in counseling by the American Counseling Association. Upon hearing this, you might think that he became a psychologist due to careful planning. But in fact, he stumbled into his career while pursuing his love of tennis.

A Long Bike Ride Leads to a Great Idea

Another example of how enjoying life can lead to life-changing experiences is found in the story Gary Erickson, the founder of Clif Bar. In 1990, Erickson was thirty-three, living in an unheated garage crowded with his skis, climbing gear, dog, and trumpets. He earned very little money, lived hand-to-mouth, and spent much of his time rock climbing in Yosemite. One of his passions was long-distance cycling. Each year he would go on cycling vacations with friends through the European mountaintops, covering thousands of miles per trip. He also raced competitively in California. Most of the racers ate PowerBars, the only energy bar that was on the market at the time.

One week Erickson's friend Jay called to see if he wanted to go for a weekend ride. Jay liked to study maps to find adventurous routes to new places, and he came up with a ride that he thought would be around 125 miles. Before departing, each of the riders packed six PowerBars. They left at dawn and cycled through the Livermore Valley, rode along the California Aqueduct, then climbed to the top of Mount Hamilton. When they had gone around 120 miles they realized that they were only a third of the way through their planned ride. Erickson had already eaten five of his six Power-Bars and his body needed fuel to continue. But when he tried to eat the sixth PowerBar, he couldn't will himself to put it in his mouth. He just couldn't tolerate its flavor and texture. Luckily, the rest of the ride was mostly downhill, and they managed to find a convenience store, where Erickson purchased a package of donuts. As they continued their ride, Erickson had an epiphany: He would make an energy bar that was better than PowerBar, one that would taste good even if you had to eat six of them. Although the two riders had to cycle late into the night, they finally made it home safely.

At the time, Erickson co-owned a bakery in Berkeley, California, that made sweets using his mother's recipes. He enlisted his mother's help, and together they began to work at creating a tasty energy bar. They experimented with different type of oats, dried fruits, and natural sweeteners. Along the way they threw out countless batches, broke mixing paddles, and burned out the motor in their KitchenAid mixer. But after six months they had what they wanted—an energy bar that was packed with nutrients, was made from healthy, unprocessed ingredients, and had the taste and texture of a cookie.

Erickson began taking his energy bars on bike races and giving them away to his friends and other riders, and the feedback was positive. In 1992, he formally launched Clif Bar. The company was an instant success, with more than $700,000 in sales its first year. For the next ten years Clif Bar grew exponentially, with $1.5 million in sales its third year and more than $20 million in sales in 1997. By 2002, Erickson had turned down an offer to sell the company for $120 million.

In his book *Raising the Bar*, Erickson notes the role that happenstance played in his success—if it weren't for his friend's adventurous ride, he never would have come up with the idea for Clif Bars. Erickson believes that the most powerful insights in his life have come from doing what he loves in challenging, uncharted terrains. His idea for Clif Bar is the perfect example of this. As a bakery owner, bike racer, and avid consumer of energy bars, he was ideally placed to conceptualize a new energy bar. But it was only through going on an adventurous ride that he was able to put it all together and recognize the possibility.

The Joyful Tipping Point

You are probably aware that your mood and productivity are impacted by the amount of sleep that you get. If you fall below a basic minimum of sleep—say, six hours a day—then at some point you are going to feel exhausted, have trouble concentrating, and function at a subpar level. Given this fact, you are probably careful (and if you aren't, you should be) to make sure that you get enough rest every night. Similarly, when you go for long periods without eating, your energy level falls and you will begin to feel lethargic and unmotivated. So you are probably careful to eat healthful foods at regular intervals. The enjoyment you experience in your life is similar to rest and food; if you don't have enough of it, then your entire life will suffer. Because of this, successful people regulate their enjoyment just as carefully as they manage their sleep and intake of food. They organize their lives to provide daily opportunities to engage in rewarding, pleasurable activities.

So how much joy do you need in your life? Let's look to research for some answers. In her book *Positivity: Top-Notch Research Reveals the 3-to-1 Ratio That Will Change Your Life,* Barbara Fredrickson suggests that to have a well-balanced, flourishing life, you need a *minimum* of three positive emotional experiences for every negative one.[6] The positive experiences need not be a big deal—it can be something as simple as going for a walk or appreciating a cup of tea with a friend. The important thing is that positive experiences occur regularly and are at least three times more frequent than negative experiences, or what Fredrickson calls the "3-to-1 ratio."

> [A] fascinating fact about people's positivity ratio is that they're subject to a tipping point. Below a certain ratio, people get pulled into a downward spiral fueled by negativity. Their behavior becomes painfully predictable—even rigid. They feel burdened—at times even lifeless. Yet above this same ratio, people seem to take off, drawn along an upward spiral energized by positivity. Their behavior becomes less predictable and more creative. They grow. They feel uplifted and alive.[7]

In her book *The Progress Principle: Using Small Wins to Ignite Joy, Engagement, and Creativity at Work*, Teresa Amabile discusses the factors that impact employee motivation and creativity.[8] She finds that the single most important factor related to employee happiness is having the opportunity to make progress at meaningful work. When people make forward strides at work that is important to them—whether completing a task, solving a problem, or writing five pages of a report—they are more positive and more creative. But when their efforts are thwarted by unsupportive environments and insufficient resources, people become negative and unproductive. Given this, Amabile suggests that to sustain motivation and performance, it is important to structure each day to include progress at work that is enjoyable and meaningful. It is not the size of the progress that is important but the frequency. Even when progress happens in small increments, it makes a huge difference in one's outlook:

> Real progress triggers positive emotions like satisfaction, gladness, even joy. It leads to a sense of accomplishment and self-worth as well as positive views of the work and, sometimes, the organizations. Such thoughts and perceptions (along with those positive emotions) feed motivation, the deep engagement, that is crucial for ongoing blockbuster performance.[9]

Although Amabile's research focuses on workplace motivation and performance, it also applies to people's overall lives. In our work with our clients we have found that the reason many people feel trapped, bitter, and hopeless is that they spend the bulk of their time fussing over trivial things and not enough time working on what matters to them. There is no better reason for being depressed than never having the chance to pursue work and projects that are meaningful to you.

Don't Let a Day Pass without Having Fun

The work of Amabile and Fredrickson points to the importance of seeking regular doses of enjoyment in your life. *Every day should include opportunities to enjoy pleasurable activities and to make progress at meaningful work.* The positive experiences and moments of progress need not be anything exceptional, but it is crucial that they occur on a daily basis.

When you include enough positive moments in your life, you cross a sort of mental tipping point and come to perceive the world in a different way. You enter into a mind-set that is flexible, confident, quick to assess situations, hopeful, and appreciative. You are sensitive to opportunities and eager to act on them. In contrast, when your experience is deficient in regular moments of joy, you are likely to have a negative outlook, feel frustrated, indecisive, unmotivated, and see no end to your present situation. You will be blind to opportunities, and when you do see them, you will be too tired and uninterested to act upon them.

Eating the Tasty Pie

Ryan recently encountered an example of the joyful tipping point while working with his client Madison. She came to see Ryan because she was having doubts about her career plans. For the last three years Madison had worked as a legal analyst at a biotech company. Her original plan had been to work for a few years before continuing on to law school, but she was finding it difficult to take the next step forward.

When Madison first walked into Ryan's office, it was obvious that she was under a lot stress. She held her body rigidly and in a monotone voice described how she was having a hard time coping with job-related stress. Her department had recently gotten a new manager, and in his introductory speech to his staff, he said that his first goal would be to cut back on the deadwood in the department. He added that he would be on the lookout for people who made mistakes and didn't carry their weight. (Isn't it amazing that there are still bozos out there who think that this is an effective way to motivate employees?)

Madison, understandably, was not encouraged by her boss's remarks, especially given that she was feeling unsure about her career choice. She had decided to pursue a career in law because it *sounded* like a good thing to do. A number of her relatives were lawyers and comfortably well off, and her parents encouraged her to become an attorney. The problem was that Madison didn't have much of a passion for law. She liked how it was analytical and provided interesting problems to solve, but it didn't get her very excited. She had never read a law book for fun, or attended a legal workshop because she was eager to learn. Her current plan to attend law school felt more like a burden than something to look forward to. She was also tied up in knots over the Law School Admission Test (LSAT), which she needed to take to apply to law school. Madison was good at standardized tests and was confident that she would get a high score on the test, but she felt overwhelmed by exhaustion and dread whenever she considered studying for it.

As Madison described her situation, Ryan noted that there was little authentic enthusiasm in her voice. He told her that although she mentioned a number of ways that she thought being a lawyer would be "interesting," it was like hearing her describe a date with someone whom she wasn't attracted to but didn't want to say anything bad about. You know, like "Well he was a very nice guy, and his table manners were excellent." Madison laughed loudly when Ryan mentioned this, giving a hint of the expressive person stifled inside her.

Ryan asked Madison about the fun things she was doing in her life, and she said that she presently wasn't doing much that she enjoyed. Most nights she was tired and cranky when she got home from work. She would play some computer games before going to sleep, only to get up the next day to repeat the same uninspiring routine. She felt guilty about procrastinating on studying for the LSAT exam, and she didn't want to commit to anything until she buckled down and got to work. She also felt so stressed out that it was starting to impact her relationship with her boyfriend. She was often impatient with him and didn't want to cuddle.

The first thing Ryan decided to do was to help Madison increase the fun in her life. He noted that it seemed like she was beating herself up over the LSAT, and asked if she might want to take a three-month sabbatical from worrying about the exam and focus instead on doing things she enjoyed.

With an obvious sense of relief, Madison agreed that this sounded like a great idea. Ryan then asked her if there were any fun things she would like to do. Madison mentioned that for a long time she had wanted to get back into acting. She described how she had begun participating in plays during grade school and continued to perform in productions throughout college. As Madison talked about her acting experiences, she spoke enthusiastically and peppered her remarks with humorous asides (not to mention a few well-placed swearwords). It was like watching an entirely different person—one who was warm, animated, and full of energy.

Ryan asked Madison if she had any ideas about how she could get involved in acting—preferably as soon as possible. She said that as an undergraduate she had participated in an informal drama group with other students. The members met weekly to work on improvisation, prepare for auditions, and act out scenes from their favorite plays. Madison knew that there were a number of people at her work who were interested in acting, and she decided to see if they would be interested in forming a drama group.

The next week at work, Madison sent out an email announcing her interest in starting a drama group, which she suggested could meet at her house. The first week, four people agreed to attend. When Madison described their meeting during her next session with Ryan, she was so excited that she was practically leaping out of her chair. She said that having such a great time had helped her see how she had lost touch with "big-smile, unadulterated fun."

As Madison started having more fun in her life, she began to see that her work wasn't very rewarding. Her interactions with clients—most of whom had violated the company's policies—were often tense and confrontational, requiring her to talk in what she called her "zombie" voice. She realized that she wanted to work in a setting where she could interact with many different types of people in a fun, supportive way. This, she saw, was unlikely to occur in the legal profession (though creative lawyers can have fun too!).

In the past Madison had considered only jobs related to the legal field. Now, with some trepidation, she began to explore farther afield. She realized that she didn't want to pursue a career that was merely "interesting." She wanted one that provided the big "wow" of excitement she experienced when working with her acting group. One of her most enjoyable job experiences was when she worked as a resident student advisor during her undergraduate years, so she began to look into jobs providing the opportunity to work with students.

After exploring many possibilities, Madison ended up accepting a job as a manager of student engagement at a major software company. In her new role, she creates programs to establish relationships with engineering students from underrepresented groups. The job offers the opportunity to tackle challenging projects, interact with business leaders, career professionals, and university faculty, and work individually with students to encourage their career growth. Madison has found that she no longer needs to be a "zombie" at work. She is now free to let her fun-loving, enthusiastic personality come out. Meanwhile, she has continued to work on acting and performing. She has recently been trying her hand at stand-up comedy, telling humorous stories about growing up in a Korean family at open-mike nights at local venues. She now sees that personal enjoyment and career growth go hand in hand. Being a foodie, she puts it this way: "In life, you want to eat the TASTY pie. And to know what pie is tasty, you need to eat lots of pie."

Tracking Your Joy

To build more moments of joy into your life—doing what makes you feel alive, appreciative, curious, and enthusiastic—it can be useful to track the ebb and flow of your emotional experiences. A number of research studies have shown that there are significant emotional, cognitive, and organizational benefits that come from journaling on a daily basis.[10] We encourage you to start a journal where you record your experiences and insights related to implementing the Do-It-Anyway approach in your life. (Throughout this book, we will introduce a number of activities that utilize your journal.) You don't need to write anything elaborate—just spending a few minutes recording your observations can be beneficial. Here are some things you might want to consider writing about each day:

- What did you do today that was a lot of fun?
- What is something interesting that you learned?
- What happened that made you appreciate your life, work, family, or friends?
- What did you encounter that made you curious?
- What did you experience that filled you with awe?
- What did you see that was beautiful or inspiring?
- What new things did you try, or new places did you visit?
- What fulfilling social interactions did you have?

Just like everything you do, you should find a way to write in your journal that is enjoyable and brings out your creativity. So let go and have fun. Come up with your own questions and exploratory practices. Try writing (and illustrating) like a crazy philosopher, wacky inventor, curious anthropologist, or compassionate humanist.

Mapping Joy

The easiest way to improve your life is to spend more time doing things that you enjoy and that result in positive experiences, and less time pursuing activities that drag you down and limit your options. You can get a better idea of the value that different activities bring to your life through an activity we call *mapping joy*. The basic idea is to create a map of the major places in your daily routine according to how enjoyable they are.

The first step is to create a map of your life. Draw a map that includes the significant places where you spend your time—for example, your home, work, gym, favorite restaurant, friend's house, local park. Don't worry about making the map fancy or true to scale. You just want to create a layout that shows the major places you frequent in a day or week. Each place can be a little circle on the map with a title. For places where you spend a significant amount of time, you may want to create larger circles broken into separate areas. For example, if at work you spend time in your office, the conference room, the cafeteria, and the product lab, you can break your work circle into four compartments. Similarly, if you spend a lot of time at home, you can break your home circle into the areas of your house (e.g., your living room, bedroom, den, and backyard).

The second step is to look through your map and consider the degree of joy you experience at the different locations. It is helpful if you attend to how you feel *while you are actually at the mapped location.* In other words, when you are at the gym, take a moment to get a read on the level of enjoyment you experiencing while you are there. Similarly, if you spend an hour at your computer surfing the Internet each night, look into how happy it makes you feel while you are doing it. Then, for each area on your map, give it a score on a scale of one to ten indicating the degree of joy you experience there, with ten representing the greatest degree of joy.

The third step is to use your map to guide you toward more positive experiences. You want to spend more time where you have a lot of fun, and less time in the areas where you feel negative and lifeless.

There are some places on your map where you have the freedom to choose if you go there or not (e.g., the yoga studio, the sportsbar where you watch *Monday Night Football*, the shopping mall that you visit on Saturday afternoons, the local coffee shop). If for any given place you feel vibrant and actively engaged while there, then you should continue going. On the other hand, if you find places where you tend to feel bored and drained, then you may want to avoid them.

When you do this activity, you may be frustrated to find that some of the least enjoyable places on your map do not feel like they are open to choice. For example, you have to go to work each day, and you may need to spend an hour commuting in your car. We must all negotiate lives filled with competing constraints and responsibilities—our careers, family obligations, and social commitments. But it is important to remember that one of your most precious gifts is the freedom to choose where you go and what you do. Your happiness and fulfillment are directly related to this choice. *If you want a successful, happy, and meaningful life, you must choose to spend your time doing things that fill you with joy.* It's that simple.

The final step in the mapping process is to use your map to introduce new areas of joy into your life. You want to be like an adventurer and look for unexplored territories that provide exciting new experiences. For example, you might note that there is a museum near your work that sounds like fun, a community center down the street that offers interesting evening courses, or a new fusion restaurant that looks enticing. When you have found some new locations you would like to explore, do it! Go there, learn, meet people, have fun, and be open to whatever happens. Once you have visited these new places, you can add them to your map. Over time, your map—and more important your life—will broaden to include a more diverse range of enjoyable settings and activities.

2

Fail Fast, Fail Often

....

We made mistakes, of course. Most of them were omissions we didn't
think of when we initially wrote the software. We fixed them by
doing it over and over, again and again. We do the same today.
While our competitors are still sucking their thumbs trying to make
the design perfect, we're already on prototype version #5. By the
time our rivals are ready with wires and screws, we are on version
#10. It gets back to planning versus acting: We act from
day one; others plan how to plan—for months.

—MICHAEL BLOOMBERG, ENTREPRENEUR AND NEW YORK
MAYOR, IN HIS BOOK *BLOOMBERG BY BLOOMBERG*[1]

A life spent making mistakes is not only more honorable,
but more useful than a life spent doing nothing.

—GEORGE BERNARD SHAW, IRISH PLAYWRIGHT AND COFOUNDER
OF THE LONDON SCHOOL OF ECONOMICS

IN THE BOOK *Art and Fear*, the artists Ted Orland and David Way-
lon share a story about a ceramics teacher who tried an experiment
with his class.[2] The teacher divided the students into two groups.
Those sitting on the left side of the studio were to be graded solely
on the quantity of their work, while those on the right, solely on the

quality. The instructor informed the students in the quantity group that a simple rule would be applied to evaluate their grades: those who produced fifty pounds of pots would get an A, those who produced forty pounds a B, and so on. For the quality group, the instructor told the students that he would assign a course grade based on the single best piece produced over the duration of the course. So if a student created a first-rate pot on day one of the course and did nothing else for the term, he would still get an A.

When the end of the quarter arrived and it came to grading time, the instructor made an interesting discovery: the students who created the best work, as judged by technical and artistic sophistication, were the quantity group. While they were busy producing pot after pot, they were experimenting, becoming more adept at working with the clay, and learning from the mistakes on each progressive piece. In contrast, the students in the quality group carefully planned out each pot and tried to produce refined, flawless work, and so they worked on only a few pieces over the length of the course. Because of their limited practice, they showed little improvement.

We like this story because it points out an important principle: successful people take action as quickly as possible, even though they may perform badly. Instead of trying to avoid making mistakes and failing, they actively seek opportunities where they can face the limits of their skills and knowledge so that they can learn quickly. They understand that feeling afraid or underprepared is a sign of being in the space for optimal growth and is all the more reason to press ahead. In contrast, when unsuccessful people feel unprepared or afraid, they interpret it as a sign that it is time to stop, readdress their plans, question their motives, or spend more time preparing and planning.

Let us ask you some questions: When was the last time you

accomplished something that you are really proud of? How did you feel in the time before you reached this accomplishment? Was it comfortable? Easy? Did you have to do things that pushed you beyond your abilities? Did you make mistakes and mess up? If you are like most people, you will probably find that the times in your life when you grew and accomplished the most are also the times when you made the most mistakes and blunders and had to overcome the greatest obstacles.

In this chapter we hope to change the way you think about failing. We want to encourage you to fail as quickly and as frequently as possible, rather than worry about doing things badly or making mistakes. We will introduce some easy-to-implement practices that will allow you to *deliberately* use your mistakes and failures to accelerate your learning and expose you to new opportunities.

Do It Badly, as Fast as You Can

When you encounter accomplishments of successful people—whether an enthralling stage performance, a beautiful work of art, an innovative business, or an ingenious invention—it can be easy to think that these accomplishments are the result of unusual brilliance and came into being perfectly formed. But the truth is that most significant accomplishments arise out of hundreds of mistakes and failures. For example, a seasoned comedian, such as Jerry Seinfeld or Chris Rock, tries thousands of hastily conceived joke ideas, most of which flop, in small clubs and venues. Only a few performance ideas, after many revisions and improvements, make their way into the polished shows presented to national audiences.

Howard Schultz's creation of Starbucks provides a good example of how success arises from many mistakes. When Schultz first formed

Starbucks, he had the idea of modeling the stores after Italian coffee shops, which would provide a new experience for customers in the United States. Although Schultz's idea was a good starting point, the Starbucks coffee shops today have little resemblance to his initial concept. In fact, many things were wrong with his idea. In the original stores, the baristas wore bow ties, the menus were primarily in Italian (and annoyed the customers for being so), nonstop opera music played in the background, there were no chairs, and nonfat milk was not served. The coffee shops of today evolved through thousands of experiments, adjustments, and revisions along the way.

Failing quickly in order to learn fast—or what Silicon Valley entrepreneurs commonly call *failing forward*—is at the heart of many innovative businesses. The idea is to push ahead with a product as soon as possible to gather feedback and learn about opportunities and constraints so that you can take the next step. This mind-set is at the heart of the brilliant work of Pixar Animation Studios. When Ed Catmull, the cofounder and president of Pixar, describes Pixar's creative work, he says it involves a process of going from "suck" to "non-suck." The moviemaking process begins with rough story boards where a few good ideas are buried amid tons of half-baked concepts and outright stinkers. The animation team then works its way through thousands of corrections and revisions before they arrive at a final cut. By giving themselves permission to fail again and again, animators weed out the bad ideas as quickly as possible and get to the place where real work can occur. As Andrew Stanton, the director of *Finding Nemo* and *WALL-E*, describes, "My strategy has always been: Be wrong as fast as we can. Which basically means, we're gonna screw up, let's just admit that. Let's not be afraid of that. But let's do it as fast as we can so we can get to the answer. You can't get to adulthood before you go through puberty. I won't get it right the first time, but I will get it wrong really soon, really quickly."[3]

Giving yourself permission to make a mess of things is particularly important if you do any sort of creative work. (We should note that all people are creative—which is to say that they live in the real world, form ideas, come up with solutions to problems, have dreams, and forge their own path; your own life is your ultimate creation.)

In her book *Bird by Bird,* Anne Lamott discusses the challenges faced in writing.[4] She says that an essential aspect of getting work done is allowing yourself to write a "really shitty first draft." You write a terrible first draft so that you can have a somewhat better second draft, and an even better third draft. As she says, "Very few writers really know what they are doing until they've done it." It is only sitting down and stringing together some words—despite not knowing what you want to write or where your narrative will go—that puts you into the place where the story can begin to unfold. This expresses an idea that is central to the Fail Fast approach: *You can't know what something is like, how you will feel about it, or what will result from it until you actually are doing it.*

Fail Fast to Learn Fast

Audience question: Hey, Louie, I started stand-up about three months ago in New York City. Can you offer any advice/tips that you knew just starting out? Maybe how to handle the New York City rooms better? I know I have to get up as much as possible, but I look up to you a lot and your work, so anything you could offer would be great. Thanks a lot.

Louis C.K.: I can't help you at all. The only road to good shows is bad ones. Just go start having a bad time and if you don't give up you will get better.

—EMMY AWARD–WINNING COMEDIAN LOUIS C.K.[5]

What do innovators like Chris Rock, Howard Schultz, and Ed Catmull have in common? They are willing to fail time and time again
in order to get their bearings, move forward, and learn. *Successful
people understand that the best way to learn about something and get good at
it is to fail at it as fast as they can.* Since every significant accomplishment is preceded by flops, bad ideas, false starts, and failed efforts,
these people are willing to fail as quickly and as often as possible to
get it out of the way. Instead of studying, preparing, and delaying so
as to avoid making mistakes, they find ways to immediately take action, create, or do something *even though* they know that their efforts
will fall short of perfection (or even minimal competency).

Since success is usually preceded by bumbling starts and botched
efforts, you can think about anything you would like to succeed at
in terms of how you must first be bad at it. You can put it in this
form: If I want to succeed at _____, I must first be bad at
_____. For example:

- If I want to be a great musician, I must first play a lot of bad
  music.
- If I want to become a successful businessman who makes
  shrewd decisions, I must first spend time making crummy
  business decisions.
- If I want to write a novel, I must first write bad fiction.
- If I want to become fluent in Chinese, I must first speak a
  lot of horrible Chinese.
- If I want to become a serious artist, I must first create
  trivial art.
- If I want to become a top commercial architect known for
  energy-efficient, minimalist designs, I must first design
  inefficient, clunky buildings.

- If I want to become a talented and courageous rock climber, I must first be an awkward timid, climber.
- If I want to have strong mathematical skills and tackle challenging analytical problems, I must first struggle with simple math exercises.
- If I want to become a great tennis player, I must first lose lots of tennis games.

We encourage you to develop a *fail first* attitude toward anything you aspire to do. Instead of treating failure as something to be avoided, strategize to find ways to make a hash of things as quickly as possible so you can learn from them.

Let's take a look at this idea in a real-life example from Ryan. In high school, Ryan heard that there was a chess club that held monthly round-robin chess tournaments at a local coffee shop. He was curious about chess, so he showed up to watch one of the tournaments. There were a dozen boards set up and about thirty players who moved from table to table. The players looked like they were having a good time, joking and chatting, while still focusing intently on their games. To Ryan, it looked like a lot of fun.

Although he knew how to play chess, Ryan was a beginner who had played only a few times. He didn't like the idea of embarrassing himself in front of the other players at the club—most of whom were older—so he decided to practice on his own before he attended the club events. He got a chess computer program and started practicing every night. The program had settings to choose the skill level, from 1 for beginner to 10 for master. The first few times Ryan played the computer, it beat him quickly, even at the novice level. After two months of practice, he reached the point where he could win about half of his games at level 5. "Well, I guess I am now half a master,"

Ryan thought to himself, and he decided it was time to try playing at the club.

When Ryan arrived for the chess tournament, he was eager to show off his chess skills. He realized that he might not be as good as the best players, but he still expected to make a grand showing by making it about halfway through the tournament before losing a game. He nervously sat down at a table with a friendly, bearded man. As the game unfolded, Ryan was slow in his moves, but he ultimately ended up winning the game. Feeling a little more confident, he moved to another table for the next round. This time the game did not go so well. Unlike the computer chess program, which always started games in the same way, his opponent began with a sequence of moves that Ryan had never seen before. As he sat there befuddled, wondering what to do, his opponent chatted with some friends who stood nearby. Ryan agonized over each move, but his opponent moved in an instant, without even needing to study the board. Ryan fell into a trap and was checkmated in short order. Deeply embarrassed, he slunk away and returned home. Later that night, while thinking about his resounding defeat, Ryan decided that he probably didn't like chess that much. Although he stopped by the chess club a few more times to observe the tournaments, he never worked up the courage to play again.

Now let's consider Ryan's experience in terms of his approach to failure. From the beginning, he was worried that he might look like a dummy at chess, especially given that most of the other players were older. He wanted to present himself as an expert, not a beginner. He therefore decided to practice on his own before he started playing with others. In doing so, he greatly limited the kinds of interactions he had and only played games with two people.

What might have happened if Ryan had sought from the beginning to lose as many games as he could? With this goal in mind, he would have started playing whenever he found the chance, whether it was with friends, strangers, or at the weekly chess club meetings. If he had lost a hundred games with other players, it is likely that he would have had a richer experience. He would have had fun meeting new people and been exposed to different styles of play. Instead of being threatened by the more skilled players, he could have seen them as potential teachers who could help him learn. They might have told him that the chess program he was using for study was quite limited and that better alternatives were available. He also would have become comfortable with losing and realized that it was just a part of the game rather than a statement about his intelligence or abilities.

Be a Beginner, Not an Expert

Nobody ever dies of making a mistake, saying the wrong thing, or acting upon a bad idea. (Well, that is assuming you're not leaping off cliffs or jumping in front of trains.) Yet living to avoid failure is a real killer—it destroys opportunities for new experiences and growth. The cruel irony of the fear of failure is that in attempting to avoid failure, people often act in ways that *guarantee* it.

Fear of failure masks itself in many disguises: laziness, jealousy at the success of others, distraction, indecisiveness, doubt, caution. When you are worried about whether you have enough talent or intelligence, you tend to engage only in things that you know you are good at and that confirm your abilities, and avoid activities that might call into question your competence or expertise. Before trying something, you ask yourself: Is this something I will be good at? Will it show how I am smart, talented, and have what it takes to succeed?

If you approach all activities as a measure of your intelligence, talent, or worth, then your overly severe attitude will limit you. Your actions will show either how you are competent or how you are not. But if you do things from the perspective of a beginner, then there are many possibilities. You may learn new things, make friends, discover something you're curious about, or just enjoy the moment. If your expectations are to try something, have fun, and see what it brings, there will always be something positive you can take home from an experience.

A general rule of thumb to the Fail Fast approach is that you should always try to act in ways that leave more options on the table. You want to have room to be surprised by life and be open to luck. By approaching things as a curious beginner, you not only put yourself in the optimum frame of mind to learn and grow, but you also open yourself to unexpected opportunities and experiences.

The benefits of focusing on learning as opposed to competence have been exemplified in the work of the psychologist Carol Dweck. In her classic research study, she had four hundred fifth-grade students complete a test composed of easy-to-solve problems.[6] She broke the students into two groups. The first group was praised on the basis of their intelligence. They were told something like "Wow, you got most of them right. You must be really smart." The second group was praised for their effort. They were told something like "Great job. You must have worked really hard."

In the second phase of the study, the two student groups were given the choice of taking two different tests. They were told that one test would have more difficult problems but they would learn a lot by doing it. The other test would include only easy problems, similar to the first test that they took. The majority of the students praised for their intelligence chose to take the easier test, whereas 90 percent of the students praised for their effort chose to try the more difficult test.

In the third phase of the study, both student groups were assigned a difficult test that included problems that were two years beyond their grade level. Most of the students failed the test. The students were then told that they performed more poorly than they had on the easier test and asked how they felt about it. The students who were praised for their effort not only performed better on the difficult test, but they also had a more positive reaction to their poor performance. They said they enjoyed working on the hard problems and wanted to take the problems home so they could practice more. Dweck summarized, "The students praised for their efforts were able to keep their intellectual self-esteem in the face of setbacks."[7]

In contrast, the students praised for their intelligence not only performed more poorly on the difficult test but also did not want to take the problems home to practice. Dweck wrote, "The students praised for their intelligence received an initial boost to their egos, but their view of themselves was quickly shaken when the going got rough."

In the final phase of the study, having artificially induced failure by giving a test beyond the students' abilities, the researchers had the students again take an easy test. The students who had been praised for working hard rebounded strongly and performed 30 percent better than they had on the initial easy test. But the students who had been praised for their intelligence did not cope well with their poor showing on the difficult test. They performed 20 percent worse than they had on the previous easy test. Dweck comments, "Emphasizing effort gives a child a variable that they can control. They come to see themselves as in control of their success. Emphasizing natural intelligence takes it out of the child's control, and it provides no good recipe for responding to a failure."[8]

The take-home message of Dweck's research is that the way that you approach challenges can have a tremendous impact on your performance. If your primary concern is to prove how smart and capable you are, then you will not only be hesitant to try things that threaten your sense of competence, but you will also perform more poorly when you do approach new activities. But if you view challenges as an opportunity to learn and grow, you will perform better, enjoy yourself more, and find ways to gain from the experience. In light of this, we encourage you to approach new activities with the mind-set of a beginner, especially when trying something that you are unsure of.

Try Things Like a Beginner

- Present yourself as a newbie who is eager to learn.
- Be playful and curious.
- Focus on learning, not on how well you can perform.
- See other people as teachers and ask for help.
- Expect to make mistakes.
- Try to discover what you don't know; reject the idea that you should appear as an expert

---

The Worst Lecturer in the Universe

A wonderful example of trying things like a beginner and failing forward can be found in the story of Helen, a university lecturer. When Helen was a graduate student in clinical psychology, she was offered the unexpected opportunity to teach an introductory lecture course in psychology. Helen was terrified by the prospect of lecturing in front of a large class, but having always wanted to teach, she decided to give it a try. The class was a disaster. Since she had to prepare on short notice, Helen had little opportunity to polish her

PowerPoint slides and practice her timing, so her lectures were often jumbled and ran over the allotted time. Although smart and articulate, Helen is soft-spoken and shy in group settings. She also has a tendency to giggle when she is anxious, which is an endearing quality when you know her personally but led to some pretty strange moments during her lectures. Helen described one class that went particularly badly. In the middle of her lecture, she discovered that she had lost the second half of her PowerPoint presentation, and in the stress of the moment, her mind went blank. She had to stumble through the remaining thirty minutes without any idea of what to say. Droves of students, in exasperation, packed up their books and marched out of the room.

At the end of the quarter, Helen received an average student evaluation rating of 1 out of 5, which was the lowest score of any instructor at the university. One student commented that Helen was the "worst lecturer in the universe."

After such a stressful first experience as an instructor, many people would probably have decided to never teach again. But instead of seeing her shortcomings as a reason to quit, Helen saw them as an opportunity to improve. As she said, "The great thing about being so terrible at the beginning is that it was so easy to get better."

Helen was offered another opportunity to teach a class over the summer. This time she had more time to prepare, and she worked to address the many problems she experienced during her first class. To keep students engaged, she added amusing stories, videos, and cartoons. To make the class flowing and flexible, she broke her lectures into shorter multipart discussions. To sustain the students' energy and attention, she came up with engaging group activities. Although Helen wouldn't call her second class a success, it was a vast improvement over her first effort.

Helen has now been teaching at the university for ten years.

Unlike many instructors who stick to teaching the same courses year after year, Helen happily agrees to teach any class that she finds interesting. She figures that the more classes in which she has a chance to do badly, the better an instructor she will ultimately be. By teaching such a wide variety of subjects, she has become skilled at mastering new material and crafting rigorous yet entertaining lectures. The students have responded to her efforts. There is usually a long waiting list for each of Helen's classes, and she is consistently ranked by student evaluations as the best professor in the university. Perhaps because of her earlier teaching disasters, this success has not gone to Helen's head. She has learned that part of the joy of being a professor is in striving to master the art of teaching, which she sees as a lifetime project. "The day I quit teaching," she said, "will be the day that I run out of ways to make my classes better."

Redefining Failure

When things don't work out the way you hoped, you can change how you feel by redefining the word "failure." Below are some examples. Can you think of others?

Failure = seeing that you are off course
Failure = realizing you need to learn more
Failure = product testing
Failure = finding out how you need help
Failure = exploring
Failure = discovering that you've been misinformed
Failure = experimenting
Failure = seeing how you need to work harder
Failure = learning that it is not your best idea
Failure = market research
Failure = prototyping

Failure Is What You Make of It

Here you might be saying: "Well, all this talk sounds nice enough, but no matter how you spin it, it's still no fun to fail." It is certainly true that no matter how positive-minded you try to be, it can be painful when things don't work out the way you want—when your application isn't accepted at an elite school, you don't get the job, your artwork isn't taken by a gallery, your business doesn't catch on, or you find that you aren't as talented as you hoped. When this happens, it is going to feel disappointing. It may make you doubt your intelligence, abilities, and ideas. That's OK. It is a short-lived pain that will go away. This is nothing compared to the fear of failure, which drains your vitality and paralyzes you from taking the actions that bring joy and meaning into your life.

It may help you to accept the unpleasantness of failure if you consider its alternative—living a stuck-in-a-rut life:

- *You always do what you already know about.* You never experience freshness and change.
- *You try only things you know you can be good at.* You don't discover your unrecognized talents and interests.
- *You don't try things that might undermine or invalidate your assumptions.* You never transcend your limiting beliefs.
- *You get involved only in things when you know you can be an expert.* You don't get help from others and experience the joy of learning.
- *When things don't work out the way you want, you take it as a sign of your incompetence and you quit.* You don't allow yourself the chance to stick with things, learn from them, build momentum, and move toward greater success.

So what can you do when you fail at something that is important to you? First, acknowledge that you did your best and that things didn't work out the way you hoped. If you want a life filled with passion and growth, then the discomfort of failure is part of it. So acknowledge your disappointment and then move beyond it.

The second thing you can do when you fail is to learn from the experience so that you can take the next positive step forward. Let's consider some ways you might do this:

- *You took action based on a bad idea or incorrect assumptions.* You can quickly move on to a better idea. You can discover lapses in your understanding or knowledge and take action to improve them. You can learn which thought process led you to form misguided ideas or assumptions, and come up with better ways to approach things in the future.

- *You tried something—perhaps committed yourself to it—only to discover that you aren't very good at it.* You get to see that your core strengths and aptitudes lie elsewhere and can move on to other options. You see that if you truly want to excel, you will have to work harder.

- *You try something and discover that you don't like it very much.* You recognize that your energy and attention can be directed toward more fulfilling activities.

Failing Forward

This is an easy-to-implement practice that will allow you to use your fear of failure as a means to take action and explore new things.

1. *Identify your fear:* Find something that you would like to try but have hesitated to do because of your fear of failure. (I want to try working as a professional photographer, but I am afraid that I might not be good enough at it to be successful.)

2. *Reverse your thinking:* Come up with a way that you can fail at it as quickly as possible. (I am going to find a setting where I can take lots of bad pictures and let people see them. I can try at my cousin's wedding, which is happening next month.)

3. *Do it anyway:* Get out there and give it a try. Make mistakes and have fun doing it. Ask others for help and feedback. (While taking pictures at the wedding, I will let people know I am a beginner and ask for comments and suggestions.)

4. *Fail forward:* Use your exploratory actions as a means to learn and discover what you need to know. (What parts of taking the wedding photographs were the most or least enjoyable? What pictures did people like or dislike? What came naturally, and what do I need to work on?)

5. *Find the Next Challenge:* Seek out the next opportunity to do things at the limits of your abilities. (Next time I will ask to take pictures at a wedding where I get paid for my work.)

3

Be Curious

· ·

*We keep moving forward, opening new doors, and doing new things,
because we're curious and curiosity keeps leading us down new paths.*

—WALT DISNEY, MOTION-PICTURE PRODUCER,
PIONEER OF ANIMATED CARTOON FILMS

It is a miracle that curiosity survives formal education.

—ALBERT EINSTEIN, NOBEL PRIZE–WINNING PHYSICIST

*I think, at a child's birth, if a mother could ask a fairy godmother to
endow it with the most useful gift, that gift should be curiosity.*

—ELEANOR ROOSEVELT, FIRST LADY, INTERNATIONAL SPEAKER,
AND ADVOCATE FOR CIVIL RIGHTS

YOUNG CHILDREN LOVE to try new things. They fiddle, poke, prod, question, and experiment to learn more about their worlds. When kids are curious about something, they don't stop to evaluate whether it suits their abilities, will result in character-forming experiences, or benefit their future career. They just find the fastest way to try it out.

As children grow older, they spend less time tinkering and exploring, and more time worrying about what they *should* do. In school, they discover that what is valued is having the right answer and looking smart, so they learn to avoid doing things at which they might not excel. They are told that people who start something and don't stick with it are quitters, so they learn to be cautious about trying too many activities. Some well-meaning parents discourage them from pursuing impractical subjects like art, music, or literature, and from this they learn to avoid activities that aren't linked to an obvious future payoff.

Given these lessons learned in childhood, it is unsurprising that many adults come to doubt the value of their curiosity. Before trying something new, they ask, "Is this something that I *should* be doing with my time? Will it benefit me? Does it really match who I am and what I want? Can I be good at it?" Ryan recently encountered an example of this in a conversation he had with his friend Marie. Ryan mentioned how he had watched a YouTube video to learn how to play a song on an acoustic guitar. Marie immediately perked up when she heard this.

"You can learn how to play guitar on YouTube?" she excitedly asked. "I should try that—I've wanted to learn guitar for years."

Ryan described how there were many free online resources for learning guitar, and offered to send her an email with a link to a YouTube channel with many excellent tutorials.

Marie thought for a while and then her face grew serious. "I don't know," she said. "I probably don't have the patience to learn guitar. I know it takes years before you get any good. And I'm so busy. When would I find the time to practice?"

Marie then described how she had a guitar that had been given to her by an ex-boyfriend. It had been collecting dust on the top shelf of her bedroom closet for the last year. She had never tried playing it because she hadn't made up her mind whether she wanted to learn guitar or not.

Marie's way of thinking about learning guitar is all too common for many of us as we get older. Marie could have picked up the guitar and strummed it a bit. She did not need to decide whether to make a long-term commitment or not. We can all learn to strum guitars guilt-free!

Curiosity-Killing Questions (and Some Counterpoints)

Will I be good at it? By trying things that you may be bad at, you stop worrying about the approval of others and focus instead on your own fulfillment and growth.

Do I have enough time? If you love something, it will encourage you to avoid unimportant activities that take up your time.

Do I have the patience, talent, intelligence? By trying it, you may find patience and talent that you didn't know you have, or you may find an important opportunity to improve.

Am I sure I want to commit to it, and if so, will it take away from other areas of my life? You don't have to commit to anything unless you really want to.

Will it cost too much? When you discover something that you are passionate about, it may inspire you to make money in new ways, or stop spending money on things you don't need.

Will people think I am silly if I get involved? Successful people often enrich their lives with interests and hobbies that appear eccentric to others. Being silly is fun.

Will it have a practical payoff? Will I meet a new boyfriend/girlfriend, develop social connections that benefit my career, learn skills that help me to earn more money, or become more healthy and attractive? It is impossible to tell where beneficial life-changing events will arise. Since you can't know in advance, you might as well spend your time having fun and trying things you enjoy.

Don't Talk Yourself Out of Life

When you judge the merits of potential activities using a cost-rewards analysis, you tend to squash your enthusiasm. You lose the incentive to experiment and explore if you must first go through a grueling evaluation process. It makes the cost of trying things too high, and you end up avoiding much of life.

A Tibetan lama came to the United States for the first time when he was in his early seventies. He had spent most of his life in an isolated monastery. He was asked what he found most surprising about life in the United States. He said nothing about the frenetic pace of life, the advanced technology, or the abundant material wealth. Instead, he spoke of something much more touching. He said what most surprised him was the way that Americans so readily cheat themselves out of the enjoyment of their lives. When people in the West are drawn to something, they often ignore their feelings or talk themselves out of them. He said that it made him want to cry to see so many people denying themselves happiness. To him, it was a great tragedy of Western culture.

Many people have fallen into the habit of doubting their curiosity and talking themselves out of pursing their passions. They fall prey to the illusion that trying something requires a commitment and long-term plan. But the truth is that life is so complex, the world so dynamic, and people so richly multifaceted, that it is often impossible to predict even the broadest outlines of how events will unfold. The one thing you can be sure of is that you will have a more fascinating and fulfilling life if you explore what intrigues you. Of course, time is limited. You can't try everything, but you can experiment with some new possibilities.

Act on Your Curiosity

One of the reasons why successful innovators, entrepreneurs, and creative artists are able to think outside the box and recognize opportunities that others can't see is that they are voraciously curious about their world and continually learn from their experiences. As Steve Jobs told *Wired* magazine, "Creativity is just connecting things. When you ask creative people how they did something, they feel a little guilty because they didn't really do it, they just saw something. It seemed obvious to them after a while. That's because they were able to connect experiences they've had and synthesize new things. And the reason they were able to do that was that they've had more experiences or they have thought more about their experiences than other people."[1]

Another reason why innovators are able to take advantage of opportunities that others are unaware of is that they continually act on their curiosity and allow it to expose them to new experiences, places, and people. Research has shown that innovative thinkers often grow up in environments surrounded by teachers, parents, and mentors who encourage them to pursue whatever they find interesting, without regard for conventional measures of achievement. This stands in contrast to most children's experience. Four-year-old children constantly ask questions, but by the time they are six, this behavior mostly disappears. We wonder if this may be due to an educational system that is geared toward conveying knowledge rather than fostering inquiry. Children quickly learn that what is valued is not curiosity but the ability to provide the right answers to the teacher's questions.

The single biggest reason why people miss out on life-changing opportunities is that they aren't looking for them. The second reason is that they see opportunities but don't act on them. Your curiosity provides a built-in mechanism for both discovering and pursuing new possibilities. When something catches your fancy, when you are filled with unexpected excitement, or you are inexplicably drawn toward a topic you know little about, trust your curiosity and allow it to propel you into action. Following the guidance of your curiosity need not entail anything dramatic. It might mean walking into a funky store you saw down the street, picking up a book at a friend's house, driving down an interesting road, striking up a conversation with a stranger, or looking up an article on Wikipedia.

Following His Nose to Do the Impossible

People who learn to pursue their curiosity expose themselves to a wide variety of experiences that can lead to unexpected outcomes. A wonderful example of this is found in the life of Bill Strickland, the founder of Manchester Bidwell, an organization that has helped thousands of inner-city kids learn career skills and go to college.

In 1963, Bill Strickland was a lost and frustrated sixteen-year-old living in Manchester, Pennsylvania, a blighted area of dilapidated row houses and weed-choked lots filled with refuse. As a young African American growing up at a time of racial strife, Strickland continually lived on the edge of violence. One morning at school, while trudging despondently down the hallway toward his homeroom, Strickland passed by the art room. It was a sunny morning and the room was filled with light streaming in from large windows. A smell of coffee was in the air and jazz music was playing in the background. Something about the light and the smell of coffee drew Strickland inside.

At the rear of the room he saw a man working with clay on a potter's wheel. He was transfixed by the rhythmic motions of the man's hands and how the clay came alive and swelled into form. The art teacher, noticing Strickland, asked if he wanted to give it a try. Strickland said yes and sat down on a stool. The teacher plopped a blob of clay before him and Strickland began to work at it on the spinning wheel. Under his clumsy touch, the clay took on a lopsided form and collapsed on its side. But this didn't matter. In that moment he knew that he had stumbled upon something special.

This experience prompted Strickland to enroll in the art class, which became the focal point of his senior year. The orderliness and calm Strickland found in the room gave him something he had never known in the streets where he lived. He had been hopeless and depressed, but the joy of working with clay helped him see what it meant to be passionately alive.

During the summer after his graduation from high school, Strickland decided he wanted to find a way to help other kids. Even though he was a marginal student who scraped by with C's, he began serving as a tutor at a neighborhood community center. His work at the center introduced him to activists and community organizers who wanted to improve Manchester. One of the people Strickland met was an Episcopalian minister, who mentioned that the church had money available for community-improvement projects. The minister asked Strickland if he had any good ideas to offer.

As he considered this question, Strickland thought about his experience working with clay and how it had helped him find a sense of purpose. He wondered if he could create a safe, nurturing place where kids could come to learn pottery and escape the violence, racial clashes, and pervasive fear outside. He proposed the idea of starting an art center, and the minister immediately liked it. With the minister's assistance, Strickland raised $25K in initial funding from the Episcopalian Church. The church also provided the use of a house where the center could be located.

The house that the church contributed was broken-down and abandoned. Strickland worked fiendishly to renovate the building, installing new bathroom fixtures, wiring, doors, windows, and drywall. When he finally opened the center, named the Manchester Craftsmen's Guild, the kids hardly noticed it. So Strickland began making presentations at churches, community groups, and neighborhood centers to try to drum up business. Finally, things started to take off. Kids began to attend the center, and those who did come got better grades in school. Parents took notice and spread the word. More students began to enroll.

As the program grew, it began to gain the notice of Pittsburgh community leaders. In 1972, Strickland was asked to take over the leadership of Manchester Bidwell, a struggling construction trade school. Strickland improved the curriculum and expanded Manchester Bidwell's offerings to include programs in chemical processing, cooking, and other trades. Industry employers, impressed with the quality of the Bidwell graduates, gave more money to the program.

Strickland's success running both the Manchester Craftsmen's Guild and Manchester Bidwell encouraged him to form a greater vision: He wanted to build a hip, creative, modern place that could provide an inspiring atmosphere for the students. In 1986, after raising $6.5 million in capital, a new 62,000-foot arts and career training center was opened, featuring expanded studios, beautiful gallery spaces, and a 350-seat auditorium.

By the late 1990s, Strickland's remarkable success at helping struggling kids to transform their lives had caught the nation's interest. He was a guest on the *Mister Rogers' Neighborhood* TV show, was appointed to the National Endowment for the Arts, and in 1996 was awarded a MacArthur Foundation genius grant.

Today, Manchester Bidwell provides training in a broad array of fields, including gourmet food preparation, medical technology, and horticulture. The organization also provides a flourishing art program, offering classes in ceramics, photography, and digital design. Around 450 teenagers from the Pittsburgh area enroll each year, of which 86 percent graduate from high school and continue on to college.

Strickland's life provides an example of how acting upon your curiosity can lead to outcomes that you never could have imagined. By following the smell of coffee into the art classroom back in 1962, he discovered his love of working with clay. And when he decided—despite his own academic struggles—to give working as a tutor a try, he met the minister who helped him start the Manchester Craftsmen's Guild.

In his memoir *Make the Impossible Possible*, Strickland says that his success in life came from following his passion, even when it was unclear where it would lead him. As he puts it: "If you're paying attention to your life at all, the things you are passionate about won't leave you alone. They're ideas and hopes and possibilities our mind naturally gravitates to, the things you would focus your time and attention on for no other reasons than that doing them feels right . . . The hard part is trusting in them as an organizing principle in your life."[2]

Five Keys to Curiosity

Because people spend much of their lives being talked out of (or talking themselves out of) their curiosity, they often lose a healthy connection to it. If you find that the strength of your curiosity has waned, here are some considerations to keep in mind:

1. *Curiosity keeps you aware and present.* Your curiosity is a kind of awareness, or intelligence, that helps you see more of

your world and recognize opportunities to explore and learn. The more you exercise your curiosity, the more you can benefit from it.

2. *Curiosity has an expiration date.* When people doubt or question their curiosity, they tend to avoid acting immediately. They might think, "I'll wait, and if I am still curious about this a week from now [or a month, or a year], *then* I will do something about it." This does not take into account how curiosity arises in a particular setting and is often associated with an action that you can do *now*. There may be a person in the room to talk to, a path to walk down, an art gallery to enter, a gadget to pick up and examine. If you wait until later, the present opportunity may no longer be available and your initial curiosity will have faded.

3. *Curiosity provides energy.* When you are curious about something, it propels you into action. Your curiosity provides the power to get you to experiment, investigate, change, and grow. Conversely, when you are lacking curiosity, it can be a struggle to take even the smallest step.

4. *Curiosity helps you learn quickly.* Your curiosity shows you the fastest, most effective way to explore things. It provides a natural way to hone in on the relevant information, skills, and actions. It says: "Try this *now*," not "Let's come up with a comprehensive five-year-plan before we proceed."

5. *Curiosity gets things moving.* Acting upon your curiosity provides a crucial first step that sets things in motion. It is a bit like freeing a ship that has been stuck in the mud— once you get things moving, all sorts of new things become possible.

Create a "Fun to Try" List

A great way to have fun and invite happenstance into your life is by pursuing new activities that you are curious about. Do you have a wish list of things you have always wanted to try? Don't let your wish list be a waiting list, but make it a *now* list! Pick something you have always wanted to try and find a simple step you can take to get going right away.

- *Learn to speak a foreign language.* Ask a friend who speaks a foreign language to say "please" and "thank you."
- *Take up Tai Chi.* Watch someone practice Tai Chi.
- *Make your own wine.* Buy a book on winemaking.
- *Learn how to paint.* Buy a kids' set of watercolors and make a mess.
- *Take piano lessons.* Try sounding out "Happy Birthday to You" on your friend's piano.
- *Go on a meditation retreat.* Visit a local temple during your lunch hour.
- *Live in a foreign country.* Visit a part of town that has a significant Vietnamese, Mexican, Chinese, etc., population, and talk to some shopkeepers about their native countries.
- *Go for a road trip across the country.* Plot an interesting afternoon drive on MapQuest.
- *Compete in a triathlon.* Jog around the block.
- *Go backpacking.* Go for a walk in the woods.
- *Perform in a theater group.* Talk to someone in a theater group.
- *Coach a kids' sports team.* Show a kid how to throw a baseball.
- *Become a pastry chef.* Buy a box of Duncan Hines cake mix and follow the instructions.
- *Go bicycling in Europe.* Go cycling in a different city.
- *Create your own board game.* Brainstorm with your kids to come up with new rules for your favorite game.
- *Learn to cultivate heirloom roses.* Plant one rosebush.
- *Write a children's book.* Make up a new story to tell your child.
- *Take up salsa dancing.* Dance along to a video on YouTube.

4

Don't Marry a Job Before
Your First Date

. . . .

Life is what happens to you while you're busy making other plans.

—JOHN LENNON, FOUNDING MEMBER OF THE BEATLES

We must be willing to get rid of the life we've planned,
so as to have the life that is waiting for us.

—JOSEPH CAMPBELL, AMERICAN MYTHOLOGIST,
WRITER, AND LECTURER

WE HAVE ALL HEARD the question "What do you want to be when you grow up?" We live in a society where you are expected to name your future occupation—and the sooner the better. At an early age, you are not only supposed to select a career but to commit to this decision for life. If you are unsure, it is seen as being wishy-washy and indecisive. Changing course is viewed as a sign of weakness or failure.

Isn't it a little crazy that you are supposed to choose and commit to a career that you have never tried out and know very little about? It's like asking you to choose your future spouse before you have gone on the first date. Yet despite this absurdity, the pressure to "decide" one's future career is pervasive in our society. There are any number of professionals who will test you, prod you, read your aura, and tell you how they can use this information to match you to a suitable occupation; and there are hundreds of books that promise that if you just determine your personality type, measure your interests, identify your calling, discover your dream, or consider your astrological sign, you will find the key to the perfect career, lifestyle, or mate.

It is time for the madness to end! To have a wonderful, fulfilling life, you don't need to define yourself as a particular type of person or decide upon a future career. In fact, it is often overplanning and unnecessary commitment that limit people's success and happiness.

Career Matching Is Silly

The idea that career success is related to choosing a future occupation and committing to it can be traced back to the work of Frank Parsons in the early 1900s. Parsons, who has been called the Father of Vocational Guidance, believed that you could identify a person's key aptitudes, interests, and personality characteristics and match those traits to specific careers. We call this view the *matching model* because it is based on the assumption that people and careers can be characterized by specific sets of features that can be matched with one another.

Perhaps you have taken a career-evaluation test. You spent an hour reading oddly worded questions and filling out your responses on a form. Then you waited eagerly to find out what your career should be. "Boy," you wondered to yourself, "should I be a stenographer, floral designer, quantum physicist, or rodeo clown?" The anticipation was scintillating. Then you got back the results of the test and . . . phhhhtttt! Whatever it described didn't sound like you at all, or was so vague as to be useless.

Like many people, Ryan took a career-evaluation test when he was in junior high school. At the time, he was reading the biography of John Muir and loved hiking in woods. The test results suggested that a good match would be employment as a park ranger. A year later, Ryan became fascinated with horse handicapping. If he had retaken the career test then, it might have suggested he become a casino dealer or statistician. The following year, Ryan got his first computer and had fun creating computer games, which he shared with his friends. A test taken then might have told him to become a software engineer.

John had a similar experience. At age sixteen, he had applied to be an "office boy" at the local Cadillac automotive dealer. He desperately wanted this job. While he was still waiting for a decision, his high school counselor gave him a career-interest inventory that said he should be an accountant. He had answered the interest inventory questions just to prove that he qualified for the job. He was not offered the job. He had no interest in accounting.

Here's the rub: People are multifaceted and have interests that are continually changing. What challenges and excites you one year may be different in the next—it may even change from day to day. So the idea that you can be described by characteristics that are stable over time is pretty silly.

Another problem with the matching model is that it assumes that occupations are tied to specific personality types and interests. So if you are rational, introverted, and mathematically inclined, then you should be an engineer; and if you are kindhearted, caring, and love animals, then you should become a veterinarian. But what if you want to be a rational, introverted veterinarian, or a kindhearted, animal-loving mathematician? If you consider any given occupation—whether it is working as a plumber, yacht salesman, small-business owner, elementary school teacher, piano tuner, writer, cardiac surgeon—you will find that it includes people with diverse backgrounds, personalities, and talents. After all, wouldn't the world be a dull place if there was a cookie-cutter stamp that applied to people and careers, so that everybody in a profession had to be identical and do the job in the same way? Thankfully, the real world is not set up this way. Each of us creates a way to live, love, and work that is our own. You don't create a satisfying life by limiting yourself to the ways you are similar to others, but by celebrating the ways that you are unique. We encourage you to ignore anyone who tries to tell you what type of person you are and what type of life or career suits you.

The matching model also fails to account for how the world is continually changing. When John was a high school athlete in Cedar Rapids, Iowa, during the 1950s, do you think a career-inventory test would have suggested that he consider getting involved in creating a virtual, video-based learning environment? When Ryan was in high school in the 1980s, would a counselor have suggested that he look into founding a business specializing in educational technology? John and Ryan did both of these things. If you look at some of the world's most vibrant, quickly growing companies—Google, Apple, Amazon, Facebook—you will find that they employ thousands of people in jobs that didn't exist ten years ago. There is no counselor, book, or test that can match you to a career that has not yet been created. Over the course of your lifetime, you will be exposed to many opportunities that will have been inconceivable earlier in your life.

Why Career Matching Doesn't Work

- Your interests are continually in flux. What you enjoy today will likely change in ten years, five years, or even six months.
- The world is evolving and new careers are available all the time.
- You are a multifaceted, unique person who cannot be matched to just one single industry or occupation.
- True joy comes from creating your own approach to life; matching your "type" to a specific career is oppressive and limiting.
- Committing to a plan makes it difficult to adapt along the way and capitalize on unexpected opportunities.

Lean Planning Is Smart Planning

When Google, one of the most successful and innovative companies in the world, has a new software service they are considering as a potential source of revenue, they find a way to get a test version into the market as soon as possible. They don't wait until they know all the features the product will need, but deliberately rush it to the public when it is still in the testing, or beta, phase of development. They do this because they know this is the best way to get valuable feedback. If the idea is terrible, they can scrap it with a minimal commitment of resources. If changes are needed, they can implement them as soon as possible, before they have committed to a particular path.

Steve Blank and Eric Ries, both serial entrepreneurs and business scholars, have studied what allows companies such as Google to succeed in today's quickly changing world. They have found that the traditional path to founding a start-up—where you define a product, create a five-year plan, secure funding, and then execute your plan—is outmoded. Exhaustive plans are usually flights of fancy that have little relationship with reality or the success of a company. The companies that succeed in dynamic marketplaces are those that rapidly develop products with minimal planning and commitment of resources.

Blank and Ries have become advocates of what they call the "lean start-up," an approach to business where the goal is to create the "minimal viable product" that can be released to potential customers to get feedback and adjust course as quickly as possible.[1] The objective is to experiment with small interactive steps in order to accelerate the rate of learning. Facebook is an example of a "lean" company that began by offering simple messaging services and then quickly evolved additional features according to the market response.

In his book *The Lean Startup: How Today's Entrepreneurs Use Continuous Innovation to Create Radically Successful Businesses,* Eric Ries provides a systematic presentation of the lean approach.[2] The book is for entrepreneurs looking to create new products or services, but it also provides a wealth of information applicable to personal career development. In the following sections we provide highlights of some of its key ideas.

Go See for Yourself

The origins of the lean approach can be traced to the lean manufacturing revolution that Taiichi Ohno and Shigeo Shingo developed at Toyota. One of its most important concepts is the Japanese phrase *genchi gembutsu*. In English, this is translated as "go and see for yourself." According to this concept, you cannot be sure about anything, truly understand any business process or problem, unless you go and observe it firsthand. It is considered foolish to take anything for granted or to rely on secondhand information.

"Go see for yourself" should be the first words out of the mouth of every career counselor. There is no way to know how you will feel about a given career until you experience what it is like firsthand. It doesn't matter how much you read, research, or ask people questions, because *those are other people's opinions, not yours.* The way to determine what you think of a given occupation is by getting as much firsthand experience as possible and coming to your own conclusion.

This brings to mind Sara, a young woman who decided she wanted to commit herself to a career in law enforcement.

A Budding Crime-Scene Investigator Visits the Lab

Sara loved reading true-life crime books and watching television programs that featured criminal investigations. She came to see Ryan, hoping to create a long-term plan to become a forensic scientist. Ryan noted that although Sara had read a lot about crime-scene analysis, it was time for her to go see for herself. Sara found a criminology class at her community college that featured a fieldwork component, where students had the opportunity to visit the county police department and observe the crime investigators at work. Sara enrolled in the course and was quite excited on the day she visited the lab. But when she got there, she hated it. It was housed in a drab, industrial building with harsh fluorescent lights. The employees seemed tired and disinterested, and interacted with one another in a hard, impersonal way. Even the smell of the place—musty, recycled air with a hint of hospital disinfectant—was intolerable. Sara found it all very depressing. Most important, she could tell that this was not the right work environment for her. She knew that she would never be happy there.

Over the coming months, Sara worked with Ryan to explore other career options. She ended up entering the field of interior design. Sara loves researching beautiful materials and finds that working with her clients matches the expressiveness of her personality.

So what if instead of seeing for herself what a crime lab was like, Sara had forged ahead with a long-term plan? She would have enrolled in a criminology bachelor's program, invested four or more years getting her degree, and then landed a job, only to discover that the occupation was ill-suited for her. Then she would have needed to restart her career explorations, or worse yet, she might have stuck with her bad decision. She could have lost a decade or more working at a job that she didn't enjoy.

Experiencing things firsthand is not only the most informative way to explore what you are curious about, but also provides one of the key ways to get exposed to opportunities you have not yet considered. So go see for yourself!

Test Your Assumptions

An important component of the lean approach is what Ries calls *validated learning*, meaning you don't act on assumptions until they have been tested. For example, let's say you own a business that manufactures high-end dog beds. You might assume that your customers prefer beds made from nonallergenic materials. In the lean start-up approach, before acting on this assumption, you would first validate (or invalidate) it through an experiment. For example, you could create two different dog beds (ideally, rapidly created prototypes requiring minimal investment)—one made from regular materials, and one from nonallergenic. Then the two dog beds could be shown to customers to see how they respond. By experimenting in this way, it not only allows you to determine if your assumption is true, but may also expose you to unexpected revelations. So you may find that customers don't care if the bed materials are non-allergenic, but they do like how synthetic fabrics are stain resistant.

In our work as counselors, we have found that people's actions are often swayed by misleading or incorrect assumptions. Some examples we have heard include:

- I can't become a doctor because chemistry classes are too hard.
- I'll never make it in that field because it is so competitive.
- I would love to be a writer (or photographer, interior designer, teacher, etc.), but it is impossible to make a living doing it.
- That's not a job that is done by women (or men).
- I am too old to get started.
- I don't have a chance because I have the wrong degree.
- I need to speak a different language or have some specialized experience under my belt.
- I'll never get into a graduate program because my grades and test scores are too low.
- Since nine out of ten restaurants fail, I don't have a chance.
- I'm not smart enough.

It's sad to see how many people limit their lives and avoid pursuing their passion because of false assumptions, especially given that those assumptions can often be disproved with a little firsthand experience. This brings to mind Jill, a woman who in her late thirties considered switching careers to become a veterinarian.

The Girl Who Was Terrified of Blood

Jill's mother owned a pet shop, and she grew up in a house filled with dogs, cats, parrots, rats, guinea pigs, and hamsters. Jill loved caring for animals, and as far back as fourth grade, she thought that she wanted to become a veterinarian. Then came high school sciences. Although she did well in her chemistry and biology courses, Jill found that she had to work much harder to get good grades in these subjects than she did in her English courses. This stood in contrast to her nerdy older brother, who breezed through his science courses without any effort. So the first negative assumption was planted: Surely she couldn't go into medicine if she wasn't supergood at sciences. After all, isn't it foolish to pursue something if you are not naturally talented at it?

Another dissuading factor related to how she reacted to blood. Whenever she saw human blood, she was nauseated and terrified. What sort of vet could she be, Jill thought, if she couldn't stomach the sight of blood?

Jill headed off to college, where she took many courses in English and the arts. Taking to heart some practical advice from her father, she ended up getting a degree in economics, which she found moderately interesting, if not scintillating. She still thought about becoming a veterinarian, but having heard many horror stories about top students who weren't admitted into veterinary programs, she felt all the more certain that it would be a hopeless pursuit for her.

After graduation, Jill worked in management consulting for a few years, and then she attended graduate school to get her MBA. Over the next decade, she worked her way up the corporate ladder in the field of investment finance. As she entered her mid-thirties, Jill started to lose steam. She tried to keep her job interesting by switching between different work groups. For a while, this kept things tolerable. But at a certain point she realized that her heart wasn't in it anymore—if it ever had been. She was a financial success and had a secure and desirable job, but she was bored and felt like her life was turning stale. In the back of her mind, she always thought that there must be work that would be more rewarding. From time to time, she still thought about becoming a vet, but she quickly dismissed this idea based on the years of additional education it would require, as well as the strong possibility that she would never be accepted into veterinary school.

When Jill turned thirty-five, she was presented an intriguing opportunity. The company she worked for was bought out, her work group was downsized, and she was offered a six-month severance package. Jill decided to accept the severance and use the time to explore different career options. She began meeting weekly with a career counselor. The counselor's first piece of advice to Jill was to stop worrying and over-rationalizing, and to start exploring whatever seemed interesting. Jill began to pursue all sorts of ideas that sounded intriguing. Because of her background in finance, she first looked into business-related possibilities. For many years she had enjoyed sewing, so she started researching a mail-order sewing company. She loved travel and languages, so she looked into what it might be like to open a travel company or start a Berlitz language franchise. She thought it might be interesting to work as a counselor, so she enrolled in a four-week training course that allowed her to work on a suicide support phone line. All of these things were momentarily intriguing, but they didn't really capture her fancy.

Although Jill enjoyed having the freedom to explore different careers, this was not an easy time in her life. For nine months she was filled with doubt, indecision, and uncertainty. She began to wonder, "Will I ever find work that is right for me?" Her greatest fear was that she would have to admit defeat and return to the lucrative, but to her dull, world of finance.

One thing Jill had always wanted to do was study French in an immersion program in France, but this always sounded expensive and impractical. Her career counselor told her, "If not now, when?" So Jill headed off to Paris for three weeks and had a wonderful experience.

After returning to the United States, Jill felt somehow changed. Her time outside the country, as well as her explorations into many divergent career possibilities, brought her to the point where she was willing to openly consider anything, no matter how far-flung. Then she finally allowed herself to try the most obvious thing: She started to volunteer at a local vet clinic. When Jill began to work at the clinic, she discovered something she never would have guessed— that when she worked with animals in a lab setting, blood and gore did not upset her. In fact, she found that working with sick and injured animals made her feel focused and engaged in a way that she had never felt before. Her worries about being afraid of blood were completely unfounded.

It was at this point that Jill finally gave herself permission to become a veterinarian. She decided that it didn't matter if she wasn't the best science student, or that it would be hard to get into vet school, or that vets made little money. When she worked in the animal clinic, she felt happy and alive, and this was what she wanted. Once she set her mind to becoming a vet, everything fell into place. At age thirty-six, she started attending community college, where she enrolled in courses in chemistry, biology, and physics. Although her science studies were difficult, years of hard work and self-discipline had taught her to be an efficient learner, and she aced all of her classes. She applied to vet school and was accepted by three out of the five best programs in the country. She graduated near the top of her class and is now a senior veterinarian at one of the largest and most advanced animal hospitals in California. Most important, she is working at a job that she loves. Her work is demanding, stressful, and insanely busy, but the days fly by with excitement, high energy, and constant learning. She is never bored.

During her career explorations, Jill followed her curiosity, traveled far afield, asked lots of questions, and learned about many different possibilities. Her journey led her back to a dream she had always held—working as a veterinarian and caring for animals. By disproving her concerns about her fear of blood, Jill was finally able to pursue this passion.

Test Your Assumptions

Do you have assumptions that need to be put to the test? Have you resisted pursuing an intriguing job or project because you feel that you are underqualified, the work is too difficult, or the field is too competitive? Have you decided not to do something because you believe you lack the necessary intelligence or talent? Why not test your assumptions before you let them stop you? Here are some ideas of how to do so:

- If you think you have the wrong educational background or work experience for a given career, try to find examples of successful people in that field with backgrounds similar to your own. If it didn't stop them, should it stop you?
- If you think something might be too hard for you, find a way to test if you are up to the task. Enroll in a difficult course or find

a way to get involved in a challenging project. Many people find that what sounds overwhelming is in fact quite manageable when they are in the process of doing it.

- People sometimes get discouraged about careers when they hear complaints from disenchanted workers—you know, those who say, "Don't ever become a teacher [psychologist, bookstore owner, musician, etc.] because everyone who does is miserable." If you have been discouraged by such negative comments, go out and find some counterexamples—people who love their job and are excited to tell you why.

- You may have been told that it is impossible to make money at a career and that to pursue it will doom you to poverty. If this concern has inhibited you, go and find examples of people in the field who, if not rich, are fiscally sound and comfortable. Would this be satisfactory for you?

- If you hear that a field is too competitive, go talk to people who are making a success of it. Find out about their background, how they got started, and what steps they took to establish themselves. Then ask yourself, "Is this something I can do?"

- If you are hesitant to pursue something because you think you may lack the necessary intelligence or talent, get to know some people who are successful in that area. Then ask yourself, "Are they really so different from me? Could I learn the skills that helped them to excel?"

- People are often dissuaded from pursuing their passion because they think that the costs will be too high—they will have to attend school for too many years, it will take too much of a financial investment, or it will be too burdensome to become professionally established. When you stop yourself from taking action because of these concerns, you are assuming that the costs will outweigh the potential joy.

- If you are worried about the years of study that will be required, visit a school, sit in on some classes, chat with students, and get a feel for the campus. Then you can ask yourself, "Would I have fun studying here for a few years?"

- If you're worried about how much money it will take, then you can look into loan programs, consider ways to lower your cost of living, or explore strategies to procure the necessary finances. Then ask, "Are the financial burdens so prohibitive that they should stop me?"

- If you think that it may take too much effort to get up to speed in a field, then meet people who are successful and ask them what it took to get established—what daily tasks were involved, what difficulties needed to be overcome, and how long it took. Ask them if they enjoyed the process. Then ask yourself, "Would I be OK with doing this amount of work to get to where I want to be?"

- If you are worried about the money and effort needed to pursue a career or project, you can test it to see if the resulting joy is worth it. Find a way to get involved in a setting related to the career or project you wish to explore. Get engaged in activities, meet people, settle into the environment, and pay close attention to how you feel. Then ask yourself, "Is the happiness I am experiencing worth the time and money it will take to get here?"

Get Going with the Smallest Investment

Lean start-ups strive to create a *minimal viable product*—one with the fewest features and the least up-front cost. The idea is to get something into a customer's hands as quickly as possible and see how they respond. Given their feedback, you can adjust course as necessary.

The idea of minimal viable product is highly relevant to career preparation. A question many people face is how much time and resources they should spend preparing for a career before they have a chance to try their hand at it. The answer is: As little as possible! We have spoken with too many people who have studied for years and invested thousands of dollars, only to later say, "If only I had known what the work was like, I never would have pursued it." (So many lawyers have told us this that we wonder if there should be a disclaimer at the top of law school applications that reads, "Warning: The practice of law is likely to be different than you think.")

The Case of the Disgruntled Chemist

A year ago, John was in England giving a keynote presentation at a career-development conference. After his presentation, a young man named Michael came up to John and said, "Boy, I wish I heard your talk ten years ago!" He then proceeded to share his story.

In the United Kingdom, adolescents are asked to decide upon a career and commit to an educational path at age fifteen. Like most fifteen-year-olds, Michael knew little about different occupations and had no clue what to pursue. He remembered how a friend once said that chemists made lots of money. Based on this, he wrote "chemist" on his career-choice card and turned it in. From that point on, he was set on the educational path to becoming a chemist. He enrolled in a science-focused high school, studied chemistry as an undergraduate at college, and then completed a Ph.D. in graduate school. After ten years of preparation, he finally began working as a chemist, and he hated it. There was nothing about the work that he enjoyed.

John asked Michael why, if he disliked working as a chemist so much, he didn't try something else. "Are you kidding me!" Michael exclaimed. "I'm not going to throw away all those years of studying for nothing."

Michael was only twenty-five years old when he spoke to John, yet he was determined to stay the course, even if it meant spending the rest of his life employed at a job he despised. Life is far too precious to waste in such a way. Before you commit to a career, find ways to learn about it as quickly as possible—volunteer, get a temporary job in the environment you are curious about (even if it is unrelated to the work you want to do), get to know people employed in the field, or shadow someone during the workday.

Avoid Perfectionism

People often resist change and progress because they want to proceed in the most professional, polished way. Before they put themselves into a situation where they might be evaluated by others, they always find one more thing to do: They need to buy an additional piece of music recording equipment, improve their product prototype, finish one more painting, take another class, improve their website, get a better business card, and so on.

An illustration of the perfectionist approach can be found in the story of Rick, a brilliant computer scientist living in Silicon Valley. Over the years, Rick has come up with many prescient ideas, but he has never been able to capitalize on any of them. This, as he with good humor admits, is because he always wants to do things as perfectly as possible. For example, long before blogging transformed the media industry, Rick came up with the idea of creating a web service that would allow people to post simple text articles on the web. He was excited about this project and dug into it with voracious energy. Working fifteen hours a day, he soon had a working prototype. But instead of putting his software online and allowing people to try it, Rick began to think that there was still room for improvement. He thought that if he could create a more optimal programming language, then his software would run more efficiently. So he began to work on creating a new server-based scripting language. Over the next four years, he got more and more mired in technical details and lost sight of his original idea. Meanwhile, other entrepreneurs began to build blogging platforms that were neither perfect nor technologically advanced. The difference was that they quickly put their flawed efforts out into the world for others to try. In doing so, they received crucial feedback, evolved their software, and made millions of dollars.

We encourage you to resist the inclination to be a perfectionist. Instead, find the cheapest, easiest thing to try that will get you into the mix of things, expose your work and ideas, and allow you to see how people respond. If you do things in this way, you will learn more quickly and be better able to adjust course. You will also have a lot more fun.

Embrace Change

In the lean approach, you develop your business through a series of incremental adjustments. Sometimes circumstances require a more radical change. You may find that you need to sell a different type of product, serve a different industry, or adopt a new business model. Such sharp changes in direction do not mean that your course of action was a mistake. It is expected that one or more significant shifts in business strategy will be required due to unforeseen circumstances. Frequently, it is by making such changes that unexpected opportunities are discovered. A classic example of this is found in Potbelly Sandwiches.

Potbelly started as an antique store in 1977.[3] At one point, the owners decided to serve sandwiches to help draw more traffic into the store. The customers proved to be more interested in the sandwiches than the vintage glass doorknobs and Tiffany lamps. Soon there were lines of people waiting for the unique sandwiches. The owners decided to change their business from an antique store to a restaurant. They added ovens for toasting sandwiches, installed booths, and began offering hand-dipped ice cream and live music. In 1996, the hugely popular sandwich joint was bought out by a new owner and expanded to more than 200 locations across the country.

It's OK to Change Your Mind

People often worry that they will look like quitters if they fail to stick to their career plans. As a result, they will stubbornly resist moving on to a more fulfilling career path, wasting years—or even decades—clinging to a job that makes them miserable.

As counselors, we have met and worked with many people who have made substantial career shifts, some of which are:

- A computer programmer who became a professional photographer
- A cancer researcher who became a yoga instructor
- An investment banker who became an illustrator
- A historian who became a coffee shop owner
- A human resources executive who became a sculpted-glass artist
- A particle physicist who became a spiritual counselor
- A real-estate agent who opened a restaurant
- A theater actor who became a clinical psychologist

- A social scientist who opened a preschool
- A driving instructor who became a mechanical engineer

None of the people we have met who changed careers expressed regret over making the switch, but many said they wished they had had the courage to do so sooner. So don't get stuck to a plan. Be ready to change course and try new things.

Discover Your Success

Through looking at the lives of thousands of people we have found that the capacity to take immediate action, learn, and change course is more important to success than any plan. We have encountered many people who have achieved phenomenal success without ever deciding what their career should be. An example of such a success can be found in the story of Jack Dorsey, one of the founders of Twitter.

As a child, Dorsey was fascinated by maps of cities, which he pinned to the walls of his bedroom. When his father one day brought home an IBM PC Jr. computer, Dorsey quickly took to it. He used the illustrating programs to create his own city maps. Then he taught himself to program so that he could create dots for trains and buses that could be moved around the streets. Moving dots around was fun, but Dorsey wanted to give them more meaning. While listening to the chatter of voices on a police scanner, he realized he could tie this information in to his program so that the movement of police cars and ambulances could be tracked throughout the city. As he worked on adding this functionality, Dorsey learned that his program was related to a field called dispatch. When studying the code of a New York dispatch software company, Dorsey found a security flaw. He emailed the company's CEO a message describing the security hole along with a simple way to fix it. This led the CEO to hire Dorsey.

In 1998, Dorsey and his boss moved to San Francisco to launch dNet, a company that provided services for dispatching couriers. They hired a CEO and raised money, but then the tech bubble burst. In a disagreement over business strategy, the new CEO fired Dorsey and his boss.

Dorsey continued to play around with computer programming, and he began to explore how computers could be used to streamline the messaging process. In 2000, he created a simple program that allowed him to send status messages from his phone and have them reposted via email to all of his friends. Dorsey's friends did not find this capability to be useful. Few of them had mobile phones, and they didn't see why it would be interesting to receive constant updates about what their friend Jack had eaten for breakfast.

As a teenager, Dorsey had loved spending time in gardens and drawing plants with a graphite pencil. He began to wonder if this hobby might lend itself to a potential career. He returned to St. Louis to study botanical illustration at the Missouri Botanical Garden. Although he fell in love with fauna of all types and enjoyed illustrating their structure and shape, he found that this was not the right career for him. Shortly after this realization, his wrist started to hurt. After visiting a massage therapist to treat his wrist, he became fascinated with the field of massage therapy. He took a thousand hours of training, received his certification, and moved back to San Francisco to start up a practice. But he quickly discovered that the city was full of massage therapists and it was next to impossible to make a living.

While working as a nanny for a friend's daughter, Dorsey began thinking about software again. He got a job at Odeo, a start-up that created software to enable podcasting. Dorsey wasn't interested in podcasting and began to have doubts about a career in programming. He thought it would be fun to create designer jeans, so he enrolled in a fashion program in San Francisco and began designing and sewing clothes. Meanwhile, a wrench was thrown into Odeo's business plans: Apple came out with iTunes, which made it easy for people to create and distribute podcasts. Odeo's products were suddenly irrelevant. The company's president asked the staff to submit new ideas for business, and Dorsey suggested his SMS-text blogging platform. His boss immediately liked the idea and granted Dorsey the resources to begin building the software. Working with other staff members, Dorsey helped create the Twitter software platform, which was released in 2006. Twitter was quickly spun off as its own company, and twenty-nine-year-old Dorsey was chosen to be the founding CEO. Five years later, Twitter has more than 200 million users and has reportedly turned down offers from Google, Microsoft, and Facebook to buy the company for more than $8 billion.

Dorsey's entrepreneurial endeavors did not stop with Twitter. One day, he was talking to his friend Jim McKelvey, a former computer programmer who had become a glass sculptor. On the day they spoke, McKelvey had lost a $2,000 sale of a glass vase because he was unable to accept payments by credit card. The two friends, who were both talking on their iPhones, began to mull over the question of why it was so hard for small businesses to process credit-card payments. This led to the realization that an inexpensive credit-card reader could be made that plugged into the iPhone. They quickly built a prototype card reader and payment-processing software and showed it to investors, who were excited by the idea. With funding in hand, Dorsey and McKelvey cofounded Square, which now makes a free credit-card reader that can be used by anyone with a smartphone. In a little over a year, the company has signed on 750,000 merchants and handled $2 billion in transactions.

Dorsey's phenomenal success came about because he avoided detailed planning. In fact, instead of "deciding" upon a particular career and committing himself to it, he was open to trying many different things over the years—programming, botanical illustration, fashion design, massage therapy. Not all of the career possibilities worked out, but he quickly transitioned to the next thing he wanted to try.

Of course, not all of us will be as financially successful as Jack Dorsey. But everyone can follow their curiosity and pursue what they enjoy. Ultimately, success comes from building a life that is right for you, not from meeting the expectations of others. This idea was captured in novelist Anna Quindlen's 1999 commencement address at Mount Holyoke College, where she said:

> When I quit the *New York Times* to be a full-time mother, the voices of the world said that I was nuts. When I quit it again to be a full-time novelist, they said I was nuts again. But I am not nuts. I am happy. I am successful on my own terms. Because if your success is not on your own terms, if it looks good to the world but does not feel good in your heart, it is not success at all. Remember the words of Lily Tomlin: "If you win the rat race, you're still a rat."[4]

The Lean Approach to Careers

The lean approach to starting a business provides a useful analogy for establishing a fulfilling career. You should strive to be lean when pursuing your career—to act, experiment, collect information, and adjust course without the need for a huge investment or long-term commitment. Here are some tips:

1. *Make the smallest viable action plan—just enough to take the next positive action.* Don't worry about making a plan for the next three months, one year, or five years; instead focus on what you can do in the next week to have new experiences and learn.

2. *Be good at taking small steps that allow you to try and learn about many things.* Learn to enjoy initiating small actions that lead to immediate feedback.

3. *Perform experiments to confirm or disprove your assumptions about occupations that you are curious about.* Don't believe what you hear about a career or what you have learned from books and television. Come up with your own experiments that allow you to find out how you feel about an occupation, how hard it is to do, how good you are at it, and so on. For example, try volunteering, enrolling in an introductory course, taking an internship, or getting a part-time job.

4. *Be prepared to change course; expect to make many small adjustments, as well as some big ones.* Don't get stuck pursuing one career, even if you have committed time and resources preparing for it. It is normal and to be expected to adjust course according to what you learn and how your interests change.

5. *Avoid big investments in education, training, and preparation until you have learned as much as possible.* Don't make a

long-term commitment until you have taken steps to try
things, test your ideas, and learn more. For example, if
you are interested in being a doctor, volunteer at a
hospital, take a chemistry course, and see how you do
on practice MCAT tests before you commit to a pre-med
plan.

6. *Keep your plans informal.* When your friends and family
ask you what career you want to pursue, resist giving a
specific answer. Instead, tell them that you are testing
out a number of different ideas (and ask for their input).
That way you can collect facts and change direction
without feeling embarrassment or being called a quitter.

5

Think Big, Act Small

. . . .

I dream of men who take the next step instead of
worrying about the next thousand steps.

—THEODORE ROOSEVELT, THE TWENTY-SIXTH
PRESIDENT OF THE UNITED STATES

When I face the desolate impossibility of writing 500 pages, a sick
sense of failure falls on me and I know I can never do it. Then,
gradually, I write one page and then another. One day's
work is all that I can permit myself to contemplate.

—JOHN STEINBECK, NOBEL PRIZE–WINNING
AUTHOR OF *THE GRAPES OF WRATH*

What saves a man is to take a step. Then another step.

—ANTOINE DE SAINT-EXUPERY, FRENCH AVIATOR,
WRITER, AND AUTHOR OF *THE LITTLE PRINCE*

IN OUR WORK as counselors, it has been our pleasure to help people accomplish many things: to create beautiful books and works of art, start innovative businesses, build organizations that tackle serious social problems, form research institutes. We enjoy the enthusiasm and passion of those who aspire to take on new challenges and change the world in positive ways. We encourage you to think big! Don't limit yourself in any way that will hold you back from what you can achieve.

Having said this, we encourage you to *find ways to act small*. Instead of defining and elaborating on all the grand things you wish to accomplish, we want you to bring your thoughts down to earth and consider what you can do in the here and now. Although ambition and planning are important, we have found that success more often comes from a series of small, seemingly unrelated steps than it does from carefully orchestrated strategies. In this chapter, we will introduce a way of using small wins—low-cost actions resulting in positive change—as a way to collect immediate rewards, have fun, and harness the power of happenstance.

Bigger Isn't Always Better

As children we were encouraged to go for big wins—to come in first in the race, be awarded the blue ribbon in the science competition, get the best grade on our exam. Because of this, many adults feel that in whatever they pursue, they should achieve the maximum honor. By making a substantial commitment of time and resources, they hope to set themselves apart and rise above the average.

Unfortunately, going for big wins often results in behaviors that get in the way of success. Let's consider an example. Allan is a thirty-five-year-old software engineer who spends long days working at his computer. He often eats fast food while sitting at his desk. Over the last eight years, he has slowly gained weight. At times he considered eating better and exercising more, but he postponed taking action for a time when he wasn't busy.

One day Allan went to the shopping mall wearing a distinctive blue T-shirt he'd received at a software developer's conference. While he was in a department store browsing for pants, he was surprised to see a portly man standing across the aisle wearing the same shirt. Then Allan realized that he was seeing himself reflected in the glass of a display case. He was shocked at the size of his belly—he was at least thirty pounds overweight.

Seeing himself in such a rotund form convinced Allan that it was time to get into shape. He did what many people do in such a situation: He decided he would go for a *big* change. He set the goal that within a year he would not only lose thirty pounds but would also complete his first marathon.

Feeling energized by his ambitious fitness goals, Allan sprang into action. There was an employee gym at the corporation where he worked, but Allan thought that it was too rinky-dink. He carefully researched local fitness clubs, read reviews, evaluated the facilities, and decided that Gold's Gym was the best option. As an indication of his commitment, he signed up for a three-year membership. He bought fancy exercise clothes and a pair of high-tech running shoes. Then he came up with a workout schedule: Each week he would go to the gym three days, run three days, and take one day off for rest.

When Allan showed up at the gym for his first workout, he was feeling tired after a long day at work. But he made himself exercise for an hour. The next day, he went for his first run. His body was aching from his workout the previous day, and he was huffing and puffing by the time he ran halfway around the block. Still, he pushed himself to walk and jog for two miles.

By the end of the week, Allan felt like he had been in a train wreck. There wasn't an inch of his body that didn't hurt. To add insult to injury, when he weighed himself on the gym scale, he found that he had *gained* two pounds. This certainly wasn't his idea of fun. Meanwhile, a challenging project came up at work. Allan decided to take some time off from his exercise program to give his body a chance to recover. One week led to two weeks, and two weeks led to five weeks. Then things really got busy at work and Allan forgot all about exercising. Two years later, he decided to cancel his gym membership.

What went wrong with Allan's plans? He didn't lack for an ambitious goal—to lose thirty pounds and compete in a marathon by the year's end. But instead of inspiring him to take action, his lofty goal offered such a distant reward that he quit when he had just gotten started. This illustrates one of the problems with going for big wins: They are often so daunting that they stop people in their tracks and discourage them from taking actions that *would* lead to real change. This is illustrated by a study led by Professor Traci Mann at the University of Minnesota, who found that, on average, the net effect of dieting is an increase in weight over a four-year period.[1]

No Pain, No Gain? Wrong!

Allan's approach to fitness reflects a commonly held assumption—that the best way to promote positive change is by pursuing difficult goals. No pain, no gain, right? This idea is often found in books on business leadership, where managers are told that they should confront employees with "stretch goals"—game-changing, difficult-to-achieve objectives. Due in part to the influence of Jim Collins, a legion of managers believe in the importance of BHAGs—big, hairy, audacious goals—that are supposed to get workers to think outside the box and reach new heights of productivity.

In his book *Good Boss, Bad Boss*, Stanford University professor

Bob Sutton says that stretch goals are often overused and counter-productive.[2] When faced with big problems that have not been broken into manageable, bite-sized chunks, people tend to be over-whelmed and freeze up. Similar views are expressed in the work of Teresa Amabile, a professor at Harvard Business School who stud-ies what makes people creative and happy at work. Amabile's re-search indicates that high-pressure work environments are often detrimental to innovation and creativity.

In an analysis of 12,000 aggregate days of employee diaries, she found that people were least creative when they struggled to meet difficult objectives.[3] Under stressful work conditions employees felt they did not have time to think deeply and incubate ideas. Amabile's research reveals that to stay motivated, people need frequent oppor-tunities to complete tasks and build a sense of forward momentum. Given this, she suggests that managers resist the illusion that big challenges spur creativity and productivity.

Another problem with pursuing big wins is that it prompts peo-ple to act without considering other available options. When you rush to set an ambitious goal, you do so based on what you already know. You don't consider the myriad things that you have not yet been exposed to. This was certainly the case with Allan, who quickly committed to fitness goals based on his previous experience (he had been a cross-country runner in high school and belonged to a gym when he was in college). If he had taken the time to explore other fitness activities (for example, joining an Ultimate Frisbee team, taking up rock climbing, or giving yoga a try), he might have found a fitness program that was fun and sustainable.

In a working paper titled "Goals Gone Wild: The Systematic Side Effects of Over-Prescribing Goal Setting," a group of Harvard researchers describe how the pursuit of big goals can degrade task performance, inhibit learning, and lead to narrow-mindedness.[4] The main problem is that by focusing people's attention on specific outcomes, goals lead to *attentional blindness*, or a lack of awareness of other important factors. As an example, the researchers point to the story of the Ford Pinto. In 1970, CEO Lee Iacocca challenged his designers with a difficult goal: to create a new car that would weigh less than 2,000 pounds, cost under $2,000, and be ready for purchase by the end of 1970. In response, the team rushed into production a car with a gas tank mounted with just ten inches of crush space behind it. It was a hazardous design, making the car prone to fires when struck from behind. Such a glaring safety consideration should have been noticed and fixed long before the Pinto made its way into production. But the managers were so focused on meeting their challenging goal that they ignored it. The end result was the creation of a dangerous clunker—both *Forbes* and *Time* magazines ranked it as one of the worst automobiles of all time—that caused twenty-seven fire deaths and was the subject of millions of dollars in lawsuits.

The problems associated with going for big wins resonate with one of the key messages of this book: *Don't overcommit.* If you get caught up pursuing a big success you want in the future—getting your diploma, being recognized as an important writer, making your first million dollars, buying your dream house, or doubling sales for your company—you can cheat yourself out of the daily pleasures and accomplishments that keep you motivated. It may also lock you into an inflexible path that is blind to other possibilities. It is a sad truth that many people who pursue long-term goals end up slaving away toward futures they ultimately don't want. As the mythologist Joseph Campbell said of the crisis faced by many at middle age, "Midlife is when you reach the top of the ladder and find that it was against the wrong wall."

Going for Big Wins Can Stop You in Your Tracks

- It makes tasks so hard that you become overwhelmed and paralyzed from taking action.
- It makes problems more complicated and confusing.
- It pushes the satisfaction of completion into the future and dampens daily motivation.
- It requires a substantial commitment of time and resources, increasing cost and risk.
- It promotes opportunity blindness—pursuing a single course of action while ignoring others.
- It gets you to do things in the most challenging way, instead of leveraging your strengths.
- It focuses on a future payoff, so that you don't benefit from incremental progress and feedback along the way.

The Power of Small Wins

The idea of small wins originated in the seminal paper "Small Wins: Redefining the Scale of Social Problems," published in 1984 by the University of Michigan psychologist Karl Weick.[5] Weick says that when dealing with complex problems, it is best to break them into bite-sized, less challenging tasks with easily achievable goals. Splitting problems into modest steps clarifies what actions should be taken, relieves doubt and uncertainty, and reduces complexity.

Weick attributes the success of Alcoholics Anonymous to the way it encourages people in the program to remain sober for just one day or even one hour, as opposed to asking them to abstain for the rest of their lives. By accomplishing successive days of sobriety, the rewards of abstinence become apparent, and long-term sobriety becomes achievable in people's minds. As Weick writes, "Once a small win has been accomplished, forces are set in motion that favor another small win."

The strategy Weick proposes consists of breaking tasks into "a series of controllable opportunities of modest size that produce visible results." A crucial word is "visible." You need to do something that effects a tangible result—something you can touch, look at, show to others, compare. Each small win sets things in motion in the world and changes your situation so that new actions become possible. Allies are discovered, resources are revealed, and new opportunities emerge. Because of this continual flux, small wins do not proceed in an obvious path toward a predetermined destination. You can't predict how small wins will combine or where they will ultimately lead. You discover where you are going only once you've arrived.

Since the publication of Weick's paper, numerous studies have highlighted the advantages of the small wins approach for taking on a broad range of challenges—such as starting high-tech businesses, overcoming depression, managing diverse workforces, and promoting innovation.

In his book *Little Bets*, Peter Sims provides many examples of innovators, such as Google founders Sergey Brin and Larry Page, Pixar Animations Studios CEO Ed Catmull, and the iconic architect Frank Gehry, who achieve great success by initiating inexpensive, low-risk actions—or what Sims calls "little bets."[6] Innovators don't make elaborate plans or focus too narrowly on specific goals. Instead, they take many small steps to test ideas, set things in play, and gather feedback. Then they quickly iterate through successive actions and adjust course as necessary. For example, Chris Rock tests out hundreds of ideas at small comedy venues in order to come up with the complex, multipart jokes included in his national performances. As Sims states, "Most successful entrepreneurs don't begin with brilliant ideas—they discover them."

The importance of using small steps as a way to build momentum is at the heart of the work of home-organizing guru Marla "the FlyLady" Cilley. Cilley is a proponent of what she calls the "5-Minute Room Rescue." The idea is that when you are faced with an overwhelming mess, you go to the room in your house that is the biggest disaster and set a kitchen timer for five minutes. You then "boogie" around and clean up as fast as you can until the timer has run down. When the five minutes are up you pat yourself on the back and stop for the day. The next day you clean for another five minutes. By repeating this routine you get in the habit of making daily progress, which will gradually allow you to overcome even the biggest mess. Cilley's humorous and down-to-earth videos have helped millions of people clean up the clutter in their lives.[7]

From Accountant to Garbageman

An example of how a series of adaptive, low-risk steps can lead to enormous entrepreneurial success is found in the story of Tom Fatjo, a serial entrepreneur who has founded fourteen companies, including waste-management giant BFI.

In 1966, Fatjo was a twenty-six-year-old accountant who was looking for a business investment opportunity. At the time, he was the homeowners association president for a large Houston subdivision that was having problems with its garbage pickup service. At an emergency homeowners association meeting, Fatjo brought up the possibility that the housing community purchase its own garbage truck. An obnoxious association member dismissed Fatjo's suggestion, saying condescendingly that Fatjo should buy a truck so that he could become their garbageman. Fatjo took this comment as a personal challenge. He looked into the refuse business and liked what he saw. It was a low-risk industry: There was always garbage to collect, so there weren't any recessions; the housing community paid its fees ninety days in advance, which would provide up-front capital; and the trucks could be easily financed and added one at a time. Thinking that owning a garbage truck or two might be a nice investment, Fatjo proceeded to purchase a truck and took over the garbage service for his community.

As an accountant, Fatjo prided himself in being methodical and analytical. His calculations told him that a 20-cubic-yard truck could collect waste for 700 homes before it would need to make a transfer to the disposal facility, which was a two-hour drive away. On his first day driving he found that he had made a serious miscalculation: The truck got full at house 220 along the route. So the first order of business was to procure a larger truck.

For the first four weeks, Fatjo drove the truck and handled the garbage himself. He had to learn on his feet, and he faced many unexpected problems. One day the compactor on his truck broke when he still had seventy houses on his route to collect. For the subsequent stops, Fatjo had to climb into the back of his truck and stomp up and down on the garbage to try to fit the extra waste, at times sinking up to his armpits in the muck.

You might think that an accountant would be appalled by a job that entailed standing in the stinky bowels of a garbage truck. But Fatjo found that he enjoyed the physical nature of the work. He liked the easy camaraderie he shared with the other drivers and was drawn to how much there was to learn about the industry. Realizing that he wanted to see where he could take his fledgling enterprise, Fatjo quit his accounting job to pursue his garbage company full-time.

After beginning with residential waste, Fatjo added accounts

servicing shopping malls and small factories. Legislation had recently been passed that tightened the regulation of refuse handling
and banned the burning of garbage. This raised the cost of disposal
from fifty cents per truckload to a few hundred dollars. Fatjo saw an
opportunity for garbage companies that could handle both refuse
collection and disposal, so he bought his own landfill. In 1968, he
received a call from Houston's mayor asking if in twelve days he
could handle the city's garbage service. Fatjo said yes and was soon
managing an additional 1,000 trucks.

   Although his business was growing rapidly in the Houston area,
Fatjo realized that he still had much to learn about the industry. He
took a three-week trip to visit garbage companies in different cities
to study their practices. During the trip, he found that there were
many small operators but no large companies that spanned multiple
cities. He also noted that the new sanitation regulations required
significant capital outlays to modernize technology, which was un-
affordable for most small companies. Fatjo saw that there was an
opportunity for a national organization that could combine the
smaller operators and benefit from economies of scale. Over the next
three years, he purchased independent operators at a rate of one per
week. By 1976, when he withdrew from BFI to run his other businesses, the company had $256 million in yearly revenues, operated
2,800 trucks in 131 different cities, and employed 7,700 workers.

   If you went back to 1966 and tried to come up with a plan to
create a national, billion-dollar garbage-management company, the
costs and risks would appear enormous, if not infeasible. But Fatjo
didn't start his company to pursue such a big goal. Instead, he tried
his hand at refuse collection on a dare, using one truck and $500.
His objective was simply to provide better garbage service for his
community and, hopefully, make some money on the side. He
wasn't even looking to quit his accounting job. The elements that

led to his company's success—improvements in operations, expansion into new markets, and capitalizing upon regulatory changes—were all discovered along the way.

Small Wins Get Your Life in Motion

- They break complex projects into simple and easily understood steps.
- They provide an ongoing sense of engagement and completion that keeps you motivated.
- They remove uncertainty and reduce stress.
- They allow you to benefit from incremental progress and feedback along the way.
- They promote immediate action based on your strengths.
- They encourage you to be flexible in your actions and to remain open to emerging possibilities.
- They promote acting based on minimal time and cost, reducing risk.
- They free you from worrying about the future so you can fully enjoy the present moment.

Do One Thing Now

It can be difficult to get started on big projects such as changing your career path, reorganizing your office, or establishing a healthier lifestyle. When you find yourself becoming paralyzed because you are unsure of how to proceed, it is time to stop worrying about your difficult goals and to focus instead on finding one small thing to do. *No matter how confused and chaotic your life may be, you can always find one positive step to take.* By taking that first step, you get things moving and open yourself to new opportunities, making it easier to take the next step.

So what next step would you like to take? It can be anything that will allow you to learn, explore, or make progress at something that is important to you. The point is to get moving and make things happen, not to strive for a significant accomplishment. The smaller and easier your action step, the better! One of the hallmarks of the small wins approach is that you often don't know where your actions will lead. So don't worry about trying to follow a linear path. Just have fun taking lots of little steps and enjoy the surprise of being led to unexpected places.

Suggestions for Action Steps

- *Keep it specific.* Your action step should be specifically defined—who, how, where, why, and when.
- *Keep it easy.* Your action step should be easy to accomplish. (If you find that you are not completing your action steps, it means you need to make them less challenging.)
- *Keep it fun.* Whatever you choose to do, it should provide the opportunity for an enjoyable, interesting experience— something you are enthusiastic about (even if you are a little nervous).
- *Keep it immediate.* Your action step should be something that you can start right away and complete in a very short time.
- *Keep it cheap.* Your action step should entail a minimum investment of time, money, and resources.
- *Keep it real.* Try to do things that entail real-world actions: Build a prototype, talk to someone, visit a location, file a document, and so on.
- *Keep it social.* Try to take action steps that include the opportunity to interact with people and gather feedback.

Examples of Action Steps

- *I will talk to a person employed in the fashion industry by Friday of next week.*
- *I will create a rough sketch of sculpture ideas and show them to my friend Suzy on Tuesday.*
- *I will write a one-paragraph synopsis of my children's book and share it with my niece on Sunday.*
- *I will show one of my photographs to an attendee at the photography workshop this weekend.*
- *On Saturday, I will get a table at the local flea market and showcase my best pottery piece.*
- *I will create a one-page overview of my leadership seminar and show it to my boss over lunch on Tuesday.*
- *By next week, I will enroll in a course on financial planning. I will talk to my friend Linda on Sunday night to tell her about my future class.*
- *By Friday I will order one book on mentoring.*
- *I will talk to my friend Paul about his experiences working as a youth counselor.*

Build on Your Strengths

Saras Sarasvathy, a professor at the University of Virginia Darden School of Business, met with the founders of thirty companies spanning a variety of industries—steel, railroad, teddy bears, semiconductors, biotech—to explore the habits and thinking styles of entrepreneurs.[8] Sarasvathy found that entrepreneurs tend to leap into action quickly by capitalizing on their current resources—their skills, knowledge, and social connections. Contrary to the stereotype of entrepreneurs being daring risk-takers, Sarasvathy's research shows that they tend to be risk-averse and do things in the way that entails the least time and cost. An entrepreneur might ask, "Am I willing to work for three days to make a prototype to show to five people?" rather than "Am I willing to commit my life savings and the next two years for the possibility of a multimillion-dollar payoff?"

A great way to get going quickly with minimal costs and preparation is by leveraging the resources and social connections that are *already present in your life*. Whom do you know who can help you, give you feedback, or introduce you to other people? Does your current work provide opportunities for exploring things you are curious about? Are you involved in social groups or hobbies that can provide a way for you to try out some of your ideas? Find a simple step you can take that is based on your current strengths and that makes the most of your present situation. For example:

- *It seems like people are always getting married at my company. I can post an announcement on the bulletin board to volunteer as a wedding photographer.*
- *My friend Steven's sister is a vice president at Random House. I will ask Steven to introduce me to his sister so I can ask her about the children's book industry.*
- *When I coached a girls' soccer team, I met a lot of the local parents. I will chat with some of the parents to ask if they have ideas about how I can start a children's theater.*
- *I am interested in exploring work as small-business consultant. I will volunteer to work on the grants committee at the artists' guild I belong to so I can find out more about the financial operations of small-business organizations.*
- *I will tell my boss about my interest in team building and ask if I can lead a brown-bag discussion on it.*

Do It! Get Going, Have Fun, and Be Aware

Whatever your action step is, go out and make it happen. Enjoy yourself and be on the lookout for unexpected experiences and opportunities. Here are some things to keep in mind:

- Appreciate whatever arises, laugh at your mistakes, and don't get caught up worrying about a specific outcome.
- Give it your best effort and be fully committed to whatever you set out to accomplish. (If you find it difficult to focus and follow through, then it may indicate that you need to choose smaller action steps.)
- Be curious and learn everything you can.
- Look for opportunities to establish meaningful connections with people. See everyone you meet as a potential friend or helper.

Celebrate Your Small Win

Once you have completed your action step, take a moment to celebrate your small win. Hurray! You did it! Enjoy the feeling of vibrancy that comes from getting out there and shaking things up. Done celebrating? Great! Time for your next small win.

The 26-Cent Sale

Emma started taking photographs when she was thirteen years old. She grew up in a rural community in northern California and loved to hike through the countryside and take black-and-white photographs of old barns and abandoned farm equipment. In high school, she built a dark room in her bedroom and learned to develop her photographs. She entered a photo of a broken-down barn in the county fair and was awarded first place.

Although Emma loved photography, she never considered it as a potential career. Following her father's advice that she should pursue a "real" occupation, she studied computer science at college. She then proceeded to spend the next two decades working as a programmer for a number of different companies.

Over the years, Emma continued to pursue her love of photography. She made the transition to digital equipment and spent thousands of dollars on cameras, computers, and printers. She would often spend thirty hours or more perfecting a single photograph. On vacations she needed an extra carry-on bag to hold her many cameras and lenses.

When Emma was in her mid-forties, she got laid off, and for the first time in her life, she found it difficult to find another job. It seemed that all the nearby companies wanted to hire young college graduates who lived and breathed technology and were happy to work fifteen hours a day. Emma, who by that time was married and had two children, wanted more from life than writing computer code. She also realized that she had grown tired of programming. The thought of working at yet another company made her feel depressed and exhausted.

For many years, Emma had dreamed of being a professional photographer. Now she decided it was time to give it a try. She came to Ryan seeking help on how to get started.

When Emma first spoke with Ryan, she had some big goals. She wanted to be a fine-art photographer and sell her prints in galleries. She thought that the best way to get started would be to create a portfolio of a hundred high-quality photographs. From these she would create a professional website that would include all of the high-tech bells and whistles—print ordering, image management, social networking integration. She figured that it would take her about four months to create the photographs and another three months to set up the website.

Noting that Emma's goal had a high cost—over half a year of work—and afforded little opportunity for social interaction and feedback, Ryan asked if there was a way that she could put together a website featuring her best photos in the next week or two. Emma was at first resistant to the idea of creating a website quickly, as she feared that it would appear unprofessional. Ryan reassured Emma that she would have plenty of opportunities to improve her website over time, and she agreed to see what she could put together quickly.

It took Emma a little over two weeks to create her website, which showcased many of the beautiful photographs she had taken over the years. She sent an email to her friends and relatives announcing the site and was thrilled by their supportive comments.

In the subsequent counseling session, Ryan asked if Emma had any ideas for ways to experiment working as a photographer. For example, could she volunteer to take pictures at a friend's wedding, or take some shots for a local business owner? Emma wasn't keen on approaching people as a volunteer, because she wanted to focus on building her image as an established fine-art photographer. But after receiving much encouragement, she gave it a try.

Over the ensuing weeks, Emma found a number of opportunities to do volunteer work as a photographer. She took shots for an advertising brochure for a local flower shop and spent a day photographing a high school judo competition. She also volunteered to take photographs for one of her daughter's friends, who needed portraits to submit with her theater school application. Emma was surprised by how much she enjoyed this work. She had always assumed that taking commercial pictures would be boring, but she found that there were interesting creative possibilities in even the simplest photograph. It was rewarding to see her pictures put to real use—her daughter's friend had been wowed by the striking portraits Emma had taken.

For her next step, Emma chose to get to know people in the local art community. She joined an artists' guild that held monthly events. The group was in the process of writing a grant to create an arts website. Emma, who had years of expertise in web design, volunteered to head the committee. Through her involvement in the artist guild, she was able to meet a number of established photographers who shared their insights about getting into the business.

Emma was intrigued by the possibility of selling her photographs via one of the many stock-photography companies. She thought that she would spend a month researching the different companies to determine the best one to work with, then take another few months putting together a portfolio to submit. Ryan asked if there was a way that Emma could get some of her photos online for sale in the next week. She agreed to find a way to do it.

During the next week, Emma found a stock-photographer site that had a simple application process and required only the submission of three evaluation photographs. She completed her application and was accepted. Although Emma was most interested in selling landscape photographs, she uploaded a variety of pictures to see what sorts of photos people would buy. One week later, Emma sold a photo of a tropical flower she had taken during a trip to Hawaii. She earned a whopping sum of 26 cents, but she was thrilled to have made her first sale. As she jokingly said, "I can at last call myself a *professional* photographer."

Emma is slowly taking on different types of paid work—portraits for a corporate yearbook, food images for a menu at a local restaurant, and a few gigs as an events photographer. She is also continuing to expand the library of stock images she lists online for sale. She loves how each project provides the opportunity to face new puzzles and learn new techniques. For an upcoming shoot, she will be trying her hand at architecture photography.

Emma hasn't lost sight of her goal of selling her fine-art photographs. She has been working on a series of black-and-white pictures of desolate landscapes, which will be included in an upcoming gallery exhibition. Although she still has a long way to go in building up her business, she is happy to be making steady progress. As she puts it, "I used to worry about impressing people and coming off as an artist. Now I just want to get to work and get something done each day."

Go for a Micro-Win

Your small win can never be too small. The faster you take action, the sooner your life will get more interesting. In this activity, we would like you to come up with a micro-win—an action step so small and easy that you can do it in the next five minutes. Here are some ideas:

- Send a short email to an old friend.
- Wash one dish in your sink.
- Go for a walk to the corner and back.
- File a document on your desk.
- Say hello to a new person.
- Read a page from the book on your nightstand.
- Meditate for one minute.

6

Be an Innovator

··

The way to get good ideas is to get lots of ideas
and throw the bad ones away.

—LINUS PAULING, NOBEL PRIZE–WINNING
CHEMIST AND PEACE ACTIVIST

INNOVATION—creating new ways to contribute value to your life and world—is at the heart of all personal success. Whether you are an engineer, salesperson, truck driver, teacher, accountant, or small-business owner, each day provides opportunities to use your inventiveness to solve problems, strategize, develop new practices, and work more effectively. Your creativity and insight are also vital to enriching your personal life. For example, you can come up with innovative ways to:

- Be a more supportive friend and coworker
- Form a unique, hybrid career that embodies your talents and passions
- Perform your daily routines—driving, preparing meals, doing your laundry—in a way that allows you to relax and recharge

- Create fun games to play with your kids
- Establish meaningful rituals to share with those you care about
- Help others to recognize their strengths and become better people
- Initiate moments of stillness and serenity that remind you of the sacredness of life

In their book *The Innovator's DNA: Mastering the Five Skills of Disruptive Innovators*, business scholars Jeff Dyer, Hal Gregersen, and Clayton M. Christensen present the results of an eight-year collaborative study in which they sought to uncover the origins of innovative business ideas.[1] The authors interviewed nearly a hundred inventors of breakthrough products, as well as the founders and CEOs of revolutionary companies, including eBay's Pierre Omidyar, Amazon's Jeff Bezos, and Salesforce.com's Marc Benioff. They also collected 360-degree data (feedback from subordinates, peers, supervisors, customers, and self-evaluations) on more than 500 innovators and more than 5,000 executives in 75 countries.

The study results show that you don't need an off-the-chart IQ or Ivy League degree to have an innovative approach to life. You just need to be willing to develop the habits of being inquisitive and actively seeking out new experiences. To illustrate this, the authors suggest that you imagine that you have a twin sibling and that you have both been tasked with coming up with a new business idea:

Imagine that you have an identical twin, endowed with the same brains and natural talents that you have. You're both given one week to come up with a creative new business idea. During that week, you come up with ideas alone, just thinking in your room. By contrast, your twin (1) talks with ten people—including an engineer, a musician, a stay-at-home dad, and a designer—about the venture; (2) visits three innovative start-ups to observe what they do; (3) samples five "new to the market" products and takes them apart; (4) shows a prototype he's built to five people; and (5) asks "What if I tried this?" and "What would make this not work?" at least ten times each day during these networking, observing, experimenting activities. Who do you bet will come up with the more innovative (and usable) idea? My guess is that you'd bet on your twin, and not because he has better natural (genetic) creative abilities.[2]

The research findings of Dyer and his colleagues, along with numerous other studies into entrepreneurial success, show that entrepreneurs don't differ significantly in personality traits or cognitive abilities from typical business executives. *But they do differ significantly in their actions.* In this chapter, we will introduce five easy ways you can take action to kick-start your innovation and initiate new possibilities in your life.

See the World Like an Anthropologist

You can see a lot just by observing.

—YOGI BERRA, FORMER AMERICAN MAJOR LEAGUE BASEBALL
CATCHER, OUTFIELDER, AND MANAGER

*Opportunities are often things you haven't
noticed the first time around.*

—CATHERINE DENEUVE, FRENCH ACTRESS

Suppose you are an alien anthropologist who has come to Earth in a rocket ship. This is your first time here, so everything is new to you.

How would you look at the world? As an innovator, this is the way you want to take in your surroundings—with fresh, curious eyes. If you want to be creative and come up with inventive ideas, you need to be an eager and active observer. In any moment, you want to be curious and surprised at the rich variety of human interactions and customs, the myriad ways that businesses work and technology is used, and how daily life is shaped by tools, technology, and media. Innovation scholar Jeff Dyer and his colleagues found that successful innovators act like anthropologists and carefully attend to contextual details of their environment and people's behaviors. Similarly, Tom Kelley, the general manager of the iconic design company IDEO and author of *The Art of Innovation*, says that the anthropologist's role is the most important source of innovation at IDEO.

Part of being a keen observer is what in Zen Buddhism has been called *beginner's mind*: You want to look out at the world as if you are seeing it for the first time. Innovation scholar Jeff Dyer and his colleagues call this "vuja de." Déjà vu, of course, is used to describe the sense that you are experiencing something that you have encountered before, even if you haven't. Vuja de, on the other hand, describes the sense of seeing something in a new and powerful way, even though you have already encountered it many times.

Examples abound of entrepreneurs coming up with transformative ideas when observing day-to-day aspects of their lives. For example, Ratan Tata, chairman of India's Tata Group, came up with the idea for the world's cheapest car on his ride home from work. Having grown up in India, where scooters serve as the primary source of transportation for millions of families, Tata had seen families crowded onto a single scooter countless times. But something in what he saw on that rainy afternoon in Mumbai jogged his thinking. He observed a man riding a scooter with an older child standing in front of him behind the handlebars. The man's wife sat behind him, holding a younger child on her lap. They were all soaked from the driving rain and obviously uncomfortable. When Tata saw this, he started to wonder, "Why can't this family own a car and avoid the rain?"

This question led Tata to wonder if it might be possible to create a "people's car" that would be affordable to lower-middle-class families. Tata brought together a small team of engineers, and after many years of trying different designs—a number of which were discarded along the way—they finally came up with the Nano, the world's cheapest car. The Nano, released in 2009 at a price of $2,200, was an immediate success, generating $200K in orders in the first few months. It was India's Car of the Year in 2010. The spark for this industry-changing car came from inquisitively observing something that Tata had seen hundreds of times before.

Another example of how observation can lead to industry-changing innovation is found in Scott Cook's creation of Intuit. One day, Cook was watching his wife work on the family's finances. She complained about how frustrating and arduous it was to keep track of everything. Cook wondered if it might be possible to use personal computers to create bookkeeping software for personal finances. This led him to launch Intuit, the maker of the QuickBooks financial software, which is now a global company with $3.5 billion in annual sales. Observation and questioning have become a standard business practice at Intuit. As Cook says, "At Intuit, we teach our people to ask these two questions as they observe: What is surprising? What is different from what you expected? That's where true learning and innovation starts."[3]

Like all positive habits, your capacity to observe is something that develops over time. When you pay more attention to your sur-roundings, the world begins to be filled with fascinating details you've never noticed before. Below is a list of things you can look for to begin developing your powers of observation.

- Your environment: What does the sky look like? Is the ground dry or wet? What noises do you hear? Can you smell anything unusual? What is the brightest color that you see?

- People: Whom do you see around you? What clothes are they wearing and what are they carrying? How are they interacting? What languages are they speaking? Do they look happy, angry, or something else? What are they doing that is common or unusual?

- Technology: What artifacts are you utilizing—computer, chair, newspaper, coffee cup, etc.—and how are they shap-ing your experience? What buildings, gadgets, appliances, home furnishings, or automobiles do you see? How do you feel about their design and visual appearance?

- Your mind and body: What is your overall mood? Are you hungry, tired, or enthusiastic? What is your posture? Are you comfortable, uncomfortable, stressed, or relaxed? Why?

- Nature: What plants, trees, and other living creatures do you see? What are they doing? What things about them are intriguing or surprising? How does their proximity affect how you feel?

- Aesthetic characteristics and meaning: What do you find beautiful and appealing in your environment? What touches you and is evocative of feeling? Can you identify an overall mood, ethos, or expressive quality in your surroundings?

The 30-Second Snapshot

A simple way to build your powers of observation is through an activity we call "The 30-Second Snapshot." The idea is to imagine that you are a supremely sensitive recording device—a kind of super-Technicolor, holographic camera—that can take in every detail of your environment. Anything that you can see, hear, touch, smell, or taste is recorded.

Spend 30 seconds recording every aspect of your setting. Scan up, down, close to you, and far away. Listen for the sounds, feel what you are touching, and breathe in the smells. Don't let anything escape your snapshot. For thirty seconds, let nothing distract you from sensing everything around you.

If you do this practice a few times a day, it will open your mind, help you to pay more attention to your world, and enhance your sensitivity to your momentary experience. It will also encourage you to be curious and notice whatever is intriguing, surprising, or touched with meaning.

Be Inquisitive

The uncreative mind can spot wrong answers,
but it takes a very creative mind to spot wrong questions.

—SIR ANTHONY JAY, ENGLISH WRITER,
BROADCASTER, AND ACTOR

I roamed the countryside searching for the answers to things I did not understand. Why shells existed on the tops of mountains along with the imprints of coral and plant and seaweed usually found in the sea. Why the thunder lasts a longer time than that which causes it and why immediately on its creation the lightning becomes visible to the eye

while thunder requires time to travel . . . These questions and other
strange phenomena engaged my thought throughout my life.

—LEONARDO DA VINCI, ITALIAN RENAISSANCE PAINTER,
SCULPTOR, ARCHITECT, AND INVENTOR

Innovators are actively inquisitive. They continually ask: Why are things this way? What is really going on here? What can be done differently?

Asking good questions can open you to surprising insights. As was said by Jonas Salk, the brilliant scientist who discovered the vaccine for polio: "You don't invent the answers. You reveal the answers by asking the right questions."

Oftentimes, it is the simplest questions that lead to great innovations. Take, for example, the case of Edwin Land, a physicist who specialized in the field of optics. While on vacation with his family, Land took a photograph of his daughter. Being a typical, impatient three-year-old, his daughter asked why she couldn't see the picture right away. This question led Land to consider why pictures couldn't be viewed immediately. Might it be possible, he wondered, to record an image onto a photosensitive surface that functioned as both the film and photo, allowing the photograph to be viewed instantly? Land's pursuit of this question led to the development of the Polaroid "instant" camera, an iconic consumer product that sold over 150 million units and transformed the photography industry. Although Land was a brilliant scientist with a deep knowledge of photographic emulsions, it was his daughter's naïve question that allowed him to break free from the assumptions of his industry and imagine a new possibility.

It is also common for innovation to arise from reframing a question about an existing problem. An example of this can be found in

Dr. William Hunter's invention of the paclitaxel-eluting coronary stent. Stents are mesh tubes surgically implanted in the arteries to keep them open. Prior to Dr. Hunter's breakthrough, stents frequently failed because scar tissue formed over the stent and reblocked the arteries. Many medical device manufacturers were pursuing the question "How can we make a better stent?" Dr. Hunter's insight came from changing this question to "What does the body do to these stents and why do they fail?" His consideration of this question led him to invent a stent coated with a drug to reduce the formation of scar tissue.

Usually, the first question people ask when faced with a problem is "How?" How can I improve my company's sales? How can I get more work accomplished? How can I save more money, lose weight, improve my golf score? When you ask a "how" question, you do so based on your existing knowledge and assumptions. For example, you might ask, "How can I establish a career that is more fulfilling?" This question may not help you much because it is likely to get you to mull over things that you *already* know—what you think you like or dislike and the types of opportunities and experiences that you have already encountered.

A good starting point when you want to inquire into a problem is to ask "what." "What" questions help you to think outside of the constraints of your current situation and explore different options. For example:

- *What* are five new things I can try to stir up my life?
- *What* if I didn't have a monthly mortgage payment or car payment?
- *What* is the biggest priority I am ignoring?
- *What* is the most important creative challenge I am facing?

- *What* is really bugging me right now?
- *What* if I were ten years younger (or twenty, or thirty)? What would I do now?
- *What* are three things I have tried that didn't work, and *what* are some ways I could do them differently?
- *What* is it that I feel I am most missing in my personal relationships?
- *What* if I had not spent the last four years getting a law degree (or engineering degree, CPA license, MBA, etc.)? *What* would I do now?
- *What* if I experienced this from the perspective of my friend, my professor, or my daughter?
- *What* if I had not already committed myself to this?
- If my life were to change in a fundamentally positive way overnight while I was sleeping, *what* would it feel like when I awoke? *What* would be different?
- *What* if I became allergic to computers (or writing business reports, attending staff meetings, filing expense reports, etc.)? *What* would I do?
- *What* if I lived in Bali? *What* would I be doing each day?
- *What* if I were struck by a magical lightning bolt that zapped away my career training and skills—my education, years of experience, multipage résumé, and contacts list. *What* would be the first thing I would want to do?
- Given that this is my life, *what* do I think I really deserve? *What* is acceptable and *what* is a waste of time?
- *What* is it that I am really afraid of? *What* do I really have to lose?

Asking "why" and "why not" questions can help you recognize hidden assumptions and self-imposed constraints. For example:

Keep an Observations and Questions Log

A great way to develop your inquisitiveness is to keep an observations and questions log in your journal. Each day, set out to find something that catches your attention or piques your curiosity, observe it closely, and then write a little bit about it. As part of this practice, you can create and collect provocative questions and ideas. Many well-recognized innovators are renowned for keeping such logs. Thomas Edison set regular idea quotas and kept over 3,500 notebooks of his ideas. Similarly, Richard Branson, the billionaire founder of the Virgin Group of four hundred companies, keeps notebooks filled with questions and observations.

Innovation has been shown to be related to multisensory stimulation. So if possible, when you observe and question your world, you should try to take in the full sense of your surroundings—what it looks, smells, sounds, and feels like. If you like to sketch, you can draw pictures in your journal to help you capture more of your experience. Or you might carry around a small camera to take snapshots. These images can then be printed and pasted into your journal. Jeff Bezos, the founder of Amazon, has his own version of this activity. He photographs "really bad innovations" as a way to help him come up with ideas for better ways to do things.

- *Why* do I feel it is too late to become a physician?
- *Why* do I have fewer close friends than I would like?
- *Why* do I feel less successful than I think I should be?
- *Why* do I have such a limited income?
- *Why* am I afraid of taking risks?
- *Why* do I care what my friends or parents think?
- *Why* do I settle for so little?
- If I hate my job so much, *why* don't I quit?
- *Why* am I always so down on myself?

- *Why* do I think I won't get accepted into school or be able to make it at some career?
- *Why* do I think I am not ready?
- *Why* do I think my business idea won't work?
- *Why* am I waiting?
- *Why* do I think I'm not good enough?
- *Why* am I afraid to change?
- *Why* do I repeat the same behaviors, even though I know they don't make me happy?

Feed Your Creativity

Invention, strictly speaking, is little more than a new combination of those images which have been previously gathered and deposited in the memory; nothing can come of nothing.

—JOSHUA REYNOLDS, BRITISH PORTRAIT PAINTER

If you want to come up with innovative ideas, it is important to stimulate your mind with material that gets you thinking in new ways. In his book *The Accidental Creative*, Todd Henry describes how creative productivity is dependent on your mental food:

> The quality of the output of any process is dependent on the quality of its inputs, and this holds true for the creative process. I call creative inputs "stimuli" because they stimulate creative thought. Despite their importance, remarkably few people are intentional about the kinds of stimuli they absorb on a day-to-day basis. If you want to regularly generate brilliant ideas, you must be purposeful about what you are putting into your head. As the old saying goes, "Garbage in, garbage out."[4]

Similarly, Jeff Dyer and his colleagues stress the importance of stimulating your mind. They provide a number of examples of great innovators who deliberately seek out places from which they can glean ideas. For example, when Steve Jobs's design team was struggling to come up with the right plastic case for the original Mac computer, Jobs went to a department store to look over kitchen appliances. He found a Cuisinart food processor that had the perfect plastic finish that could be used on the Mac. In another instance, Jobs walked through the company parking lot to look at the finish of different cars. In studying the trim of a Mercedes-Benz, he came up with an improvement for the Mac's metal-case design.

What mental food do you find most energizing? Do you start bubbling with ideas after a trip to a modern art gallery, browsing at the hardware store, walking through a tech conference, looking at flowers at the arboretum, or meandering through the local flea market? Are you inspired after listening to a science program on NPR, reading a biography, watching a documentary at the local indie movie theater, or spending quiet time meditating at home? Have fun and experiment to discover the places and activities that leave you feeling fresh, enthusiastic, and creative.

The design firm IDEO keeps a "Tech Box" that holds hundreds of high-tech gadgets, beautifully designed household objects, imaginative toys, and whimsical consumer products. When they are in the process of brainstorming a design problem, they reflect upon the articles in the box to help them break free from their current thinking patterns and to form new ideas and associations. Similarly, you can create your own "ideas box" filled with things that jog your mind—photographs, magazine articles, clever gadgets, inspiring quotes, silly toys. When you are in need of creative inspiration, you can take out your box and mull over its contents.

Another way to stimulate your creativity is by reading books and

magazines about provocative designers, scientists, artists, and thinkers. If you spend a few minutes reading an interesting book or article
before you begin your work, it will seed your mind with fresh ideas
and stimulate your own inventiveness. A fun and inexpensive way to
expose yourself to a broad range of written resources is to set aside
an afternoon to browse at your local bookstore.

Be a Relentless Learner

I began my education at an early age—
in fact, right after I left college.

—SIR WINSTON CHURCHILL, BRITISH PRIME MINISTER
AND NOBEL PRIZE–WINNING AUTHOR

Creative activity could be described as a type of learning process
where teacher and pupil are located in the same individual.

—ARTHUR KOESTLER, HUNGARIAN-BRITISH
AUTHOR AND JOURNALIST

Take a few moments to consider the following question: *When did*
you learn the things that really matter to you and have been most important
in determining the course of your life? If you are like most people, some
of the most important things you have learned were encountered
outside of the classroom. It is impossible to predict what new skill or
understanding will prove essential to opening future opportunities.
In fact, the most pivotal knowledge often seems unremarkable at the
time it is learned. Key innovations that redefine entire fields often
draw upon wisdom gleaned from seemingly unimportant experiences. For example, Johannes Gutenberg used his knowledge of
wine presses to build a printing machine capable of mass-producing
texts. Charles Eames, the creator of the iconic Eames chair, learned

how to mold plywood while working at a naval shipyard and later applied this knowledge to the design of modern furniture. Steve Jobs, well known for his ability to connect diverse ideas and experiences, was inspired to create the advanced typography for the Macintosh computer because of a calligraphy course he took for fun ten years before.

As human beings, we don't just learn skills that allow us to excel at our careers. We also learn many things related to enjoying our lives and growing as people—how to be a good friend, spouse, parent, and community member; how to enjoy simple pleasures and not get sidetracked by petty annoyances; how to build upon our strengths to contribute to others. This learning, too, often occurs unexpectedly in everyday places. In his doctoral studies at Stanford, Ryan examined the lives of spiritually committed people to see how their deepest values developed over time. He found that the insights that were most influential in shaping people's spiritual lives often arose in seemingly mundane moments. For example, people reported experiencing transformative insights while having a quiet dinner with friends, sitting on an international airline flight, or stumbling upon a deer in the woods.

When you realize that the most important learning can happen anywhere and at any time, it encourages you to value whatever you are doing and to always be open to unexpected discoveries. It also changes your perspective on taking risks and the possibility of failure. Since there is always something to learn, it means that you can take something away from every situation, regardless of the outcome. Even, or especially, in moments of personal hardship or loss, there are things that can be learned that will help you grow as a person and improve your life. A wonderful example of this can be found in the story of Ram Dass, a spiritual teacher who studied in India in the 1960s and published the seminal book *Be Here Now.* In

1997, when he was sixty-six years old, Ram Dass had a severe stroke and nearly died. After the stroke, he suffered from expressive aphasia, which made it difficult to come up with the correct words when he spoke. This was particularly challenging, given that he was a public speaker known for his eloquence.

When Ram Dass was interviewed while struggling through his painful rehabilitation, he said that his stroke provided the opportunity to better understand his spirituality and recognize where he needed growth. "I had been superficial and arrogant," he said, "and the stroke helped me to be humble. I had gotten power from helping people and now I need help for everything. That was the grace. The stroke happened to the ego, and when I could witness the pain, my life got better." Now in his eighties, Ram Dass continues to speak to and inspire audiences around the world.

Seek Out Opportunities to Learn

If you want to be successful, you should always be on the lookout for opportunities to learn and grow. One obvious place to put this into practice is in your current job. You can get involved in projects that allow you to acquire new skills and learn about different technologies, industries, and work practices.

You should also strive to embrace learning opportunities outside of work. Whether you participate in social groups, help run a community organization, volunteer at your local school, or belong to a kayaking club, look for chances to get involved in activities and projects that expose you to new challenges and experiences.

One last way you can embrace learning is by deliberately setting aside time to pursue activities that introduce you to new skills and areas of knowledge. For example, each month you can set aside a "learning day," when you spend time exploring activities and subjects you find intriguing.

Get Outside the Box

We don't know who discovered water,
but we know it wasn't the fish.

—MARSHALL MCLUHAN, CANADIAN COMMUNICATIONS
THEORIST AND SOCIAL REFORMER

Luck, it is said, is about being at the right place at the right time. But how do you know where the right place is, and when you should go? As with all matters of happenstance, you can never know for certain. No one is going to put up a sign that reads, "This is the right place. Be here on Wednesday at 3:22 p.m."

Innovation, like luck, is dependent on being present and ready to act at the right time and place. You are more likely to come up with transformative ideas when you are doing things out in the world—trying new activities, exploring unfamiliar places, meeting people—than when you are at home watching TV on your couch. An important aspect of becoming an innovator is learning to act outside the box—to step out of your usual haunts, habits, and thinking patterns to embrace new possibilities.

Business scholar Jeff Dyer and his colleagues found that successful innovators deliberately pursue activities that take them outside their physical and intellectual borders. For example, innovators often seek out opportunities to live in different countries and cultures. The researchers found that the more countries a person lives in, the more likely she will generate innovative products or businesses. People who live in a foreign country for at least three months are 35 percent more likely to start a business or invent a product. Similarly, CEOs who have had at least one international assignment deliver stronger financial performances than CEOs without such experience.

The benefits of diverse experiences also apply to working in different industries. The more industries a person works in, the more likely she is to become a successful innovator. Working in diverse environments presents opportunities to experience different business processes, communication styles, corporate cultures, and products. Such a rich and varied background helps one to look at problems from many angles and come up with ideas and strategies that transcend any single perspective.

Getting outside the box is especially important if you are involved in a creative endeavor. Whether you are composing music, writing stories, inventing widgets, or designing a new business product, it is easy to get excited about your ideas and develop tunnel vision that is oblivious to real-world considerations. Creative people often work independently, which can isolate them from encounters that help to develop their vision. So as a creator, it is important to find ways to venture outside of your usual workplace. For example, if you are starting a new business, you should seek out potential clients and tell them about what you plan to create (or better yet, show them a prototype of your product or service). You can get feedback and see if your product or service has features that people want, and what aspects of it are the most and least compelling. By getting outside the box and talking to others, you can quickly explore the real-world validity of your ideas. You also open yourself to unexpected opportunities—people, resources, and possibilities you hadn't considered—that can help you promote your creative work.

One way to enhance your creative potential is by getting outside of your usual physical boundaries. Try working in a different location, eat lunch at a new restaurant, travel to (or better yet, live in) a foreign country, attend a cultural event in an unfamiliar setting, or go to a museum or park you have not yet visited. When you expose yourself to new places, it helps you break free from your current thinking and envision new ideas. The design team at Daimler provides a telling example. When trying to come up with a breakthrough in automobile aerodynamics, managing engineer Dieter Gürtler had his team go to a local museum of natural history to watch fish for the day. The team observed the boxfish, talked with fish experts, and came up with a concept car design that mimicked the size and skeletal structure of the boxfish. This new design afforded substantial reductions in weight and air drag.

Another way to foster innovation is to seek out skills and knowledge outside of your current range of experiences. If you are an engineer, take a class in art; if you are employed as a business analyst, try your hand as a volunteer career counselor; if you work at a computer in an office, take up carpentry. Read books and magazines on unfamiliar topics, attend conferences on subjects you know little about, and pursue classes and workshops that help you develop new physical skills.

Perhaps the most powerful way to initiate transformative ideas is by interacting with people outside your usual social network. Seek out relationships with people in different careers, who are older or younger than you, who live in different neighborhoods, or who have a different life focus.

Map Your Luck

Innovation, like luck, is related to activity and change. You are more likely to come up with transformative ideas and encounter new opportunities when you are trying things, visiting places, meeting people, and challenging yourself than if you are repeating familiar routines. If you want to be an innovator, you need to continually find ways to get outside the box—or to step outside of your usual thinking patterns and behaviors.

The basic idea of the exercise "Mapping Your Luck," which is similar to the "Mapping Joy" exercise in chapter 1, is to identify areas of repetition and sameness in your life and to replace them with activities that bring new experiences and interactions. Here is the process, step by step:

1. Reflect on the last month of your life and look at where you spend your time. For example, you might want to consider:
   - Where you eat your lunch
   - Whom you talk to throughout the day
   - Where you go on weekend mornings
   - Where you shop for groceries
   - What you do first thing in the morning, or right before you go to sleep at night
   - Where you go on vacation
   - What books you read
   - What shows you watch on TV
   - What neighborhoods you visit
   - What gym you attend (and the routine you follow while there)

2. Make a "map" of your life that breaks up your day/week into the places where you spend your time. Don't worry about making the map fancy or true to scale. You just want to create a layout that shows the major places you

frequent in a day or week. Each place can be a little circle on the map with a title.

3. Take your map and evaluate each spatial region according to how "lucky" or "fresh" it is—how much newness, growth, and unexpected opportunities you encounter when engaged in that region. Assign a number from 1 to 10, with 1 meaning stale and boring, and 10 meaning that it is associated with creative ideas and unexpected opportunities.

4. Identify areas on your map that have low scores, and come up with fun new things you would like to try instead.

5. Do it! Replace the luckless regions of your life with the new activities and experiences.

7

Overcome Analysis Paralysis

Each indecision brings its own delays
And days are lost lamenting over lost days.
What you can do or think you can do, begin it.
For boldness has magic, power, and genius in it.

—JOHANN WOLFGANG VON GOETHE, GERMAN WRITER,
ARTIST, AND POLITICIAN

A centipede was happy—quite!
Until a toad in fun
Said, "Pray, which leg moves after which?"
This raised her doubts to such a pitch,
She fell exhausted in the ditch
Not knowing how to run.

—KATHERINE CRASTER, POET

JASON GREW UP in rural northern California in a family that was not big on traveling. A day trip to nearby San Francisco was treated as a grand adventure, requiring the sort of detailed planning one might expect for an approach on the summit of Mount Everest. No one in the family had ever traveled internationally.

During his senior year in college, Jason developed a yearning to travel abroad. He purchased a number of travel books and studied potential destinations. After four months of research, he decided that he wanted to go to Prague. At first, he thought about traveling for a few weeks, but after some consideration, he thought that it would be a more meaningful experience if he lived in Prague for a year and studied the language. This became a more extensive trip that entailed much more preparation. Jason purchased every guidebook on Prague he could find and carefully researched the hotels, restaurants, money-exchange locations, language schools, and rail and bus systems. Wanting to know more about the culture, he bought translations of popular Czechoslovakian novels to read. There was one big problem with Jason's travel plans—the more time he spent researching, the more remote and impossible the trip seemed. He ultimately got so bogged down in all the details that he lost his motivation to go and ended up scrapping the idea. He planned himself out of doing.

Many of us are like Jason. We are great analyzers. We enjoy coming up with plans, resolutions, to-do lists, and goals. Although we are masters at analysis, we are less skilled when it comes to boldly engaging in the key actions that lead to real change. You might say that we have Ph.D.s in planning and kindergarten educations in *doing*.

Too Much Thinking Can Stop You in Your Tracks

In his book *The Paradox of Choice*, Barry Schwartz provides many real-world examples of how exposure to excessive information can inhibit people's actions.[1] In a research study exploring how the availability of different choices impacts consumer purchases, two tables were set up in a grocery store to allow people to taste jam. One table had six varieties of jam and the other had twenty-four. You might think that having more types of jam to try would result in more purchases. But the opposite was true. The table with six jams ended up having ten times as many sales as the other table. When faced with too many choices, consumers were overwhelmed and passed.

When people must select from a number of choices, they are likely to get confused and choose the most familiar option, even if better alternatives are available. This tendency is illustrated in a research study created by the physician Donald Redelmeier and psychologist Eldar Shafir that explored how physicians make medical decisions.[2] One group of doctors was presented with the case of a sixty-seven-year-old patient with chronic hip arthritis. The patient had been given drugs to reduce the pain, but the treatment had been ineffective. The physician was told that a decision had been made to refer the patient to orthopedics to undergo a hip replacement, a highly invasive surgery with a long recovery time. Subsequent to this referral, it was discovered that there was a pain-treatment drug that had not yet been tried. Should the physician still send the patient over for surgery, or should the drug be tested first? When presented with the case, 47 percent of the physicians recommended prescribing the drug before resorting to surgery.

A second group of doctors was presented with the same case study, except in this version, they were told that two untried pain-treatment medications had been discovered. They were asked if they recommended proceeding with the referral for hip replacement, or if they thought one of the two drugs should be tried first. Now, if you are a patient facing an expensive, dangerous surgery, you would be happy for the opportunity to try out any viable alternative before going under the knife. One drug to try would be great, and two would be terrific. So you would expect that physicians presented with the case that had more untried drugs would be more likely to postpone surgery until drug treatment had been given a chance. But the opposite was the case. When presented with two drug choices, fewer physicians (28 percent) recommended delaying surgery to try either of the drugs. The researchers concluded that the additional choices increased the decision difficulty, making the physicians more likely to stick with the existing plan to opt for surgery.

Research by the psychologists Anthony Bastardi at Stanford University and Eldar Shafir at Princeton University highlights another characteristic of analysis paralysis.[3] In a paper aptly named "On the Pursuit and Misuse of Useless Information," the researchers described a series of studies that explored how the availability of nonessential information influences people's decision making. In one study, the researchers had university students evaluate whether an applicant should be accepted to Princeton University. One group of students was presented with an applicant who played varsity soccer, had supportive letters of recommendation, and was editor of the school newspaper. The applicant had a combined SAT score of 1250 and a high school B average. Given these conditions, 57 percent of the study participants said that the student should be accepted.

A second group of study participants was given the same applicant with a slight variation. They were told that there was a discrepancy in the applicant's file related to the grade average. The guidance counselor's report indicated a B, whereas the school office reported an A. The student participants were told that the school was checking on the record and the correct grade would be reported in a few days. Given this, the student evaluators were asked whether they should immediately admit the applicant, reject the applicant, or wait for further clarification on the grades. Most of the participants (74 percent) opted to wait for the correct grade. Those who chose to wait were then told that they had been notified that the grade average was B. Since this is the same grade average that was provided for the applicant in the first study group, where the majority of the participants chose to accept the applicant, you might expect that most would decide to accept the applicant in this case as well. But the majority (54 percent) now thought that the applicant should be rejected; waiting for the grade average made it the focal point of their decision. The study shows that when people are presented the opportunity to delay making a decision by pursuing additional information, they will readily do so; and when this information is obtained, it is often overvalued, resulting in poorer decisions.

Sorting through excessive information doesn't just befuddle you. It is also likely to wear you out. Numerous research studies have shown that making decisions can sap away energy necessary for initiating action. For example, psychologist Kathleen Vohs at the University of Minnesota and a group of colleagues explored how decision making impacted people's performance on subsequent tasks.[4] They had participants engage in a choice task—for example, choosing between different colored pencils, T-shirts, or college courses to take. Then they had the participants engage in a second task that required self-control, such as seeing how long they could keep their hand submerged in unpleasantly cold water. Study participants who did not first engage in a decision-making task were able to keep their hands in the water for a longer period of time than those who had previously made decisions.

In another study, the researchers examined how choosing between different options impacted people's subsequent ability to solve math problems. Participants who engaged in a decision-making task before working on math problems performed more poorly and gave up more quickly than participants who had not previously made decisions. The researchers concluded that making choices depletes people's energy, making them less able to initiate actions and exert self-control.

In summary, research tells us that unnecessary thinking and analysis can stop you in your tracks. The more time you spend collecting information and making choices:

- The more confused and hesitant you will become
- The more likely you will be to stick with the status quo and ignore better options
- The more likely you will be to allow trivial factors to bias your behavior
- The less energy you will have to take action and persevere in the face of challenges

If you want to be a doer—a person whose life is filled with meaningful experiences, diverse opportunities, and continual learning and growth—then it is essential that you not deplete your confidence and energy by overthinking your opportunities.

Shrink the Decision

Most of us are taught that when deciding upon a potential course of action—whether to take up piano, go to grad school, or vacation in New Zealand—it is best to think things through carefully before taking action. For example, if you are deciding whether to apply for an intriguing job you heard about, you might consider:

- Whether the work will be rewarding
- If the responsibilities will match your skills (which is often just another way of worrying about the potential for failure)
- If there will be room for professional development
- If you will make enough money
- If significant life adjustments (relocating, changing schedules, etc.) will be required
- If you are interested enough in the job to want to commit to it
- If leaving your present job is wise, in view of the economic outlook

The problem with doing an exhaustive analysis when deciding whether or not to act is that you make your choices more costly and complicated than they need to be. For example, if you are thinking about applying for an interesting job, you need only ask yourself if you are intrigued enough to submit an application—an investment of an hour or so of time. You don't need to decide in advance whether you want to commit to the job or figure out all the ways that doing so might impact your financial security and happiness. If you unnecessarily worry about such long-term implications, you are likely to end up so confused and exhausted that you won't do anything.

The way to avoid getting bogged down by big decisions is to shrink them to a more manageable size. Instead of worrying about all the ways that some dramatic move may impact the next month, year, or five years of your life, come up with a simple, exploratory step you can take. Then ask yourself, "Am I willing to try this so that I can find out more?" Even when facing complex choices that have significant ramifications for your future, you can usually still find a low-cost step to take. The story of how John came to work at Stanford provides a wonderful example of this.

Is It Time for Some Sun?

When John was an associate professor at Michigan State University, he received an unexpected letter from Stanford University. It announced that John was one of the candidates who would be coming to interview for a faculty position in the School of Education. The letter stated the date that John was expected to be present and said that his travel costs would be reimbursed. John had not applied for this position and was somewhat taken aback by the letter's presumptive tone.

At the time, John was delighted with his life. He was working with a dynamic group of scholars and engaged in interesting research projects. He was well liked by the department and had recently received a promotion. He and his wife had established roots in the community, purchased a home, and had a baby on the way. The last thing on his mind was starting a new job somewhere else.

When John received the unexpected letter and had to decide whether to attend the interview, he could have made it into a big decision. He could have pondered the implications of uprooting his family and moving to an unfamiliar place, the difficulty of starting off in a new university department, the potential impact on his research and professional collaborations, and whether he would be as happy teaching at a private university. But John didn't bother thinking about any of these things. It was a cold and dreary midwestern December, and the question that he asked was "Do I want to take a free vacation in sunny California?" The answer to this question was an easy "yes."

Shrink the Decision

When faced with a tough decision—e.g., whether you should accept a job, move to a new city, or commit to a long-term project—find an easy exploratory step you can take that will allow you to gather more information and broaden your perspective. Then ask yourself, "Am I willing to take this step to find out more?"

BIG DECISION	SHRINK THE DECISION
Do I really want to switch careers?	Am I willing to talk to a person who switched careers?
Do I want to go back to working full-time?	Am I willing to spend an afternoon in a full-time work environment to see how I feel while there?
Do I really want to commit to learning piano?	Am I willing to try one lesson to see how much I enjoy it?
Am I sure I want to go back to graduate school?	Am I willing to sit in on one class?
Do I really want to join a church?	Am I willing to attend a church event and meet some of its members?
Do I want to start dating again?	Am I willing to meet someone for coffee?
Is this the person I want to settle down with for the long term?	Would I like to see him/her again?
Should I go into business for myself?	Am I willing to go to a trade conference to see if I come upon any intriguing opportunities?

When John went to Stanford, he was impressed by the vision of the department and felt an immediate rapport with the faculty. The dean said that they were interested in having John come to do research in counseling. This was a novel idea for John. In his current faculty position, he was able to perform research only in traditional educational psychology. In hearing the dean describe the new position, John realized that it was exactly what he wanted to do. He also loved the beautiful campus and the sleepy rural town of Palo Alto (how things have changed!). And a few days of sun wasn't so bad either.

John returned home and spent some time talking to his colleagues at Michigan State University about what they thought of the opportunity. Some thought that John should stay put. Others said that if he was offered the job, he would be foolish not to accept it. (Those who recommended that John accept the position all asked that he put in a good word for them for any upcoming Stanford posts. This provides an example of how the advice people give is sometimes more about what *they* want than what is best for you.) John ended up being offered the position and accepting it, and it proved to be a positive career move.

Say Yes to Opportunity

Situations in life often permit no delay; and when we cannot determine the course which is certainly best, we must follow the one which is probably the best . . . This frame of mind freed me also from the repentance and remorse commonly felt by those vacillating individuals who are always seeking as worthwhile things which they later judge to be bad.

—RENÉ DESCARTES, *DISCOURSE ON METHOD*

When people are choosing whether to do something or not—should they enroll in graduate school, take up tango lessons, join the Peace Corps—they will often compare the pros and cons of taking action. If the positives outweigh the negatives, then they will choose to give it a go; otherwise they will hold steady. The problem with guiding your actions in this way is that you are hardwired to have a negativity bias. People are better at recognizing risks than they are at identifying opportunities, place a higher premium on potential losses than they do on equivalent gains, and react more strongly to negative stimuli than they do to positive ones.[5] As a result, it is much easier for us to find reasons to say "no" to action than to find reasons to say "yes."

A simple way to overcome your negativity bias is to apply what we call the "One Yes Trumps Three No's" rule. The idea is that when you are considering whether to do something or not, give each positive reason three times as much weight as each negative. (We should stipulate that there are some things that really are bad ideas—for example, playing shuffleboard on the freeway, or investing your life savings in Chia Pets—so you should probably only apply this rule in circumstances where there is no significant threat to your health and livelihood.) Suppose you are thinking about enrolling in a photography class. The course sounds as if it will be fun (positive), but it is offered at a location that is far from your house (negative) and at an inconvenient time (negative). Your inclination is to pass on the class, but then you remember the "One Yes Trumps Three No's" rule, so you decide to enroll.

Another problem with weighing the pros and cons when determining a course of action is that you can evaluate only what you already know. We are quite adept at identifying potential risks, which we have personally encountered or heard about secondhand (e.g., all those "helpful" friends who, upon hearing about your interest in starting a business, recite the statistics about small-business failures). But we can't consider unexpected opportunities, because they are unanticipated.

You can encourage yourself to say "yes" to opportunities by giving a bonus to any activity that is likely to introduce you to happenstance—new experiences, learning, perspectives, people, or places. For example, let's say a business acquaintance learns of your interest in social entrepreneurship and asks if you would be willing to give a presentation at his company. At first you are excited about the chance to give a talk on your favorite topic. But then you start to think it over. You don't have any PowerPoint slides prepared, so it's going to be a lot of work (negative). You would also like to brush up on some of the recent news, which you couldn't possibly do by next week (negative). But then you think of how the class will allow you to meet new people and do something that you haven't tried before (happenstance bonus!), so you decide to give it a go.

Consider the Cost of Saying No

When it comes to weighing the pros and cons of potential courses of action, we often don't take into account the default outcome—what will happen if we choose to do nothing. Sometimes the biggest risk is the future that you will end up with if you are unwilling to change:

- If you are feeling reluctant to attend a social event, think about continuing to feel isolated and lonely.
- If you are feeling too insecure to apply for a job, consider remaining with your current occupation for a year, five years, or perhaps for life.

- If you are hesitating to take on a challenging project, think about never having the chance to learn anything new.
- If you are worried about introducing yourself as a beginner, think about how it will feel to never become an expert.
- If you resist trying a fun new activity because of the time commitment or cost, think about how it will feel to continue to spend night after night watching TV and surfing the web.

Inspired by Her Annoying Boss

Megan had a secure job working as a contract manager for a construction company. For years she had dreamed of forming her own company, and in preparation she had gotten her contractor's license and formed a legal corporation. But her anxiety over the risk and uncertainty of owning her own business had always stopped her from quitting her job.

Megan's boss was a fierce taskmaster who castigated his employees whenever they socialized at work. But despite banning chitchat from office interactions, he always felt the need to talk about his own personal life, prattling on and on about the fancy parties held at his waterfront home, the recent pooping trends of his poodle, and his thirty-two pairs of designer shoes.

When Megan was taking steps to quit her job and began to feel paralyzed by fear, she would imagine having a conversation with her boss five years in the future. He would march into her office and say, "Did I show you my new badminton shoes? They're Prada." Imagining having to stomach her way through such conversations for years on end helped Megan to have the wherewithal to quit her job and strike out on her own.

Jump on a Springboard

Remember how Jason talked himself out of traveling to Prague? About ten years later, he was invited to visit a friend who was traveling in Beijing. By that time, Jason had gone on a few international vacations and realized that the key to traveling abroad is purchasing a ticket. Once you do that, everything else falls into place. Without much ado, he bought a ticket on China Air, got an expedited visa, and in ten days was on a plane to Beijing. He had such a fantastic time in China that he ended up staying there for five weeks.

Jason's approach to his trip to China provides an example of what we call *jumping on a springboard*. When you find yourself in a confusing situation with many possible choices to consider, sometimes the best thing to do is to find a key step you can take that will simplify things and move them forward. In the case of planning a vacation, buying a ticket is the springboard, because once you have scheduled your flight, everything else can be planned around it— booking hotels, arranging transport, planning an itinerary, and so on. By focusing on the main task at hand and immediately acting on it, you keep yourself from getting bogged down in endless, unnecessary analysis that depletes your motivation and kills your momentum.

Although it is easy to be indecisive and wimp out when it comes to our own aspirations, most of us will hold firm when we make a promise to others. Because of this, the best springboard actions are those that entail some sort of external commitment to others— scheduling a meeting time, making a reservation, signing up for a course, paying for the first month's membership, making a promise to a friend.

Jump on a Springboard to Leap Ahead

- You want to talk to your boss about your getting a promotion and taking on a leadership role on larger projects. For the last few months, you have been worrying about the best way to approach the conversation. How can you be assertive without overstating your case? What is the best way to showcase your contributions to the company? How should you respond if your boss reacts in an unsupportive way? Trying to answer all these "analysis" questions can block you from taking action.

  Springboard Action: Schedule a time to meet with your boss.
- Your house has gotten to be a cluttered mess. You have tried unsuccessfully to get yourself to tidy things up by writing a to-do list and scheduling time to clean, but you never stick to your plans.

  Springboard Action: Invite friends over for a dinner party at your house in two weeks.
- You are trying to plan a camping trip with the family, but you are bogged down with all the decisions that need to be made—where to go, for how long, what camping supplies you need, who can water your plants while you're away, how to keep the kids happy (and from driving you crazy).

  Springboard Action: Make a reservation at a campground.
- Your garage has become so clogged with junk that there is no room for your car. You dread sorting through the mess and have been fretting over it for months.

  Springboard Action: Schedule a truck from the Salvation Army to come pick up your extra stuff next Saturday.

- You have been developing a workshop on financial management for nonprofits. You have put in tons of time, but you are having trouble wrapping things up into a final presentation. There always seems to be one more section to improve or one more topic that needs to be included.

   Springboard Action: Offer to give your talk at a local nonprofit at a specific date and time.

- You are a budding visual artist who is struggling to put together a portfolio of your best work.

   Springboard Action: Rent a booth to showcase your work at an upcoming art fair.

- For the last year you have wanted to start a coaching practice, but you never seem to muster the energy to get started.

   Springboard Actions: Sublet an office for two days a week to meet with potential clients.

- Your business has grown and you need to hire an assistant. For the last few months, you have been thinking about the best way to bring someone onboard and what kind of project to start them on.

   Springboard Actions: Place an advertisement for an assistant on a job board.

If You Rent It, They Will Come

Back in 2005, before the advent of the iPad and Android tablets, Jim had an idea for a new consumer electronics product. As a dedicated amateur photographer, he had dozens of memory cards lying around, each holding thousands of photographs. There was no easy way to keep track of all the photos and view them. Given that flash-memory storage was getting cheaper by the day, he wondered if he could create a slim, portable device that offered enough digital storage to hold a complete library of personal photos, along with a high-end LCD on which they could be viewed.

Jim was not the type to sit around noodling over things. Ten years before, he had cofounded 3Ware, a hardware manufacturing company that produced disk controllers, which ended up being bought out for $150 million. After Jim sold his interest in his company, he began searching for his next venture. He decided to go ahead and build his photography device and see where it might lead. The only problem was that he found that he was getting bogged down in various tasks needed to get under way—researching the core electronic components, finding oversees suppliers, designing the hardware and software architecture, identifying marketing channels. Not to mention raising the funds needed to launch the business.

Finding that he was spinning his wheels in endless research and decision making, Jim decided to take a decisive step to move things forward. He rented an office on a street in downtown Palo Alto near the Stanford University campus—a location that had already hosted a number of fledgling start-ups. His thinking was that if he provided a space for his idea to take form, then he could build momentum around it. Sure enough, once he got his office, things began to happen. An engineer who used to work at Jim's previous company stopped by to visit, and upon examining a wire-strewn circuit board on Jim's desk, he became so excited by the project that he agreed to sign on as the company's lead designer. Jim invited friends in the tech industry to come by, and one of them suggested he meet with the president of a local flash-memory manufacturing company. Jim met with the president, who liked the idea and pledged a million dollars in seed funding to get things under way.

Working around the clock, it took about three months for Jim and his engineer to create the first working prototype of their photograph storage device, which was housed in a chunky case and had a rudimentary user interface. A more streamlined prototype followed two months later. Jim showed the prototype to purchasing agents at big-box consumer electronics stores and got great feedback. The next step was to raise $10 millions to ramp up to actual production. And here is where things fizzled. Jim pitched his business to dozens of venture capital firms, but although a number of them expressed interest and asked him back for multiple discussions, none of them was willing to sign a check. Ultimately, Jim decided to throw in the towel and move on to his next idea.

In Silicon Valley, failure is often the pathway to success. The more quickly and frequently you fail, the more likely you are to stumble upon the killer idea that *does* launch into the stratosphere. Jim could have easily spent a year hemming and hawing over whether or not to develop his idea. Instead, he acted decisively and rented an office to get things rolling. By doing so, he was able to get other people on board, raise seed funding, and build a prototype. He learned about electronic supply agreements, was granted a patent on a flash-memory aggregation, and got firsthand experience designing a consumer electronics product. He had an exciting year filled with learning and personal growth.

After throwing in the towel on his photography device, Jim quickly moved on to other things. He spent a year as a Sloan Fellow at the Stanford University School of Business, and he is now working as vice president and general manager of a cloud computing company. He has no idea where he will be five years from now. But wherever he is, he won't be sitting still.

Jump on a Springboard

Is there something you know that you would like to do, but you have gotten bogged down in preparation and planning? Come up with a springboard action—a key first step you can take to simplify your situation and get things rolling. *Then do it!*

8

Stop Resisting and Start Living

···

*Whatever you can do, or dream you can, begin it. Boldness
has genius, magic, and power in it. Begin it now.*

—W. H. MURRAY, MOUNTAINEER AND AUTHOR

*All worthwhile people have good thoughts, good ideas, and good
intentions, but precious few of them ever translate those into actions.*

—JOHN HANCOCK, SIGNER OF THE DECLARATION
OF INDEPENDENCE

*There are those of us who are always about to live. We are waiting
until things change, until there is more time, until we are less tired,
until we get a promotion, until we settle down—until, until, until.
It always seems as if there is some major event that must
occur in our lives before we begin living.*

—GEORGE SHEEHAN, BESTSELLING AUTHOR OF
RUNNING & BEING: THE TOTAL EXPERIENCE

THINK OF A time in your life when you were feeling happy, enthusiastic, and full of energy. Now consider what you were doing. Our
guess is that you weren't sitting at home eating Häagen-Dazs and
watching reruns of *Friends*. If you are like most people, the times in

your life that have been the most vibrant and meaningful were when you were engaged in exciting projects, taking on new challenges, learning fascinating things, immersing yourself in creative expression, or nurturing a significant relationship.

Although most of us recognize that success and happiness come from taking action to embrace the opportunities in our lives, we often have trouble getting ourselves in motion. We allow our doubt, indecision, and fear to bring us to a halt and keep us stuck in place. To help you understand why this happens, let us introduce you to the archenemy of action: *resistance*.

Resistance: The Voice That Says "Don't Do It"

As a biological organism, you are hardwired to seek familiarity and certainty, and to avoid risks and the unknown. When you stray from the familiar, your brain sends out a warning message that goes something like this: "Danger ahead . . . put on the brakes . . . retreat!" The message is usually composed of a negative emotional response (fear, doubt, confusion, ambivalence, discomfort) along with a rationalization as to why you shouldn't act (you are too busy or unprepared, the time is not right, you are likely to fail). We call this pernicious little voice that talks you out of living your life "resistance."

Resistance tends to be the most powerful and persuasive when you are facing situations that can result in significant change in your day-to-day life:

- Contemplating a change in career path, especially if it entails new skills and education (e.g., quitting work as a lawyer to become a teacher)

- Working on creative projects (writing a screenplay)
- Beginning a spiritual pursuit (taking up daily meditation)
- Considering a potential long-term commitment (getting married, having a child, moving to a new city)
- Engaging in projects with an uncertain payoff (enrolling in graduate school, starting a business)
- Interacting with people or social groups that challenge your established sense of self (starting again as a beginner, joining a drama club)
- Increasing your level of physical activity (jogging after work)
- Altering deeply ingrained habits (cutting your TV watching, reducing the amount of sweets you eat)
- Improving your home or work environment (organizing your office, cleaning your garage)

In order to get you to retreat to safer ground, your resistance exaggerates dangers, downplays positive possibilities, says that you are tired, weak, and unskilled, argues that the timing is terrible, and complains that there is no point in trying because you are doomed to fail. Your resistance is, in short, a big fat liar that will say anything to discourage you from doing what it deems to be risky!

In his book *The War of Art*, the novelist Steven Pressfield discusses the many ways that resistance inhibits people's lives—especially those who pursue creative endeavors.[1] Pressfield characterizes resistance as a sort of diabolical demon that deliberately thwarts people's efforts to pursue what is meaningful:

Have you ever brought home a treadmill and let it gather dust in the attic? Ever quit a diet, a course of yoga, or a meditation practice? Have you ever bailed out on a call to embark on a spiritual practice, dedicate yourself to a humanitarian calling, commit your life to the service of others? Have you ever wanted to be a mother, doctor, an advocate for the weak and helpless; to run for office, crusade for the planet, campaign for world peace, or to preserve the environment? Late at night have you experienced a vision of the person you might become, the work you could accomplish, the realized being you were meant to be? Are you a writer who doesn't write, a painter who doesn't paint, an entrepreneur who never starts a venture? Then you know what resistance is.[2]

. . .

Resistance cannot be seen, touched, heard or smelled. But it can be felt. We experience it as an energy field radiating from a work-in-potential. It's a repelling force. It's negative. Its aim is to shove away, distract us, prevent us from doing our work . . . [3]

. . .

Resistance will tell you anything to keep you from doing your work. It will perjure, fabricate, falsify; seduce, bully, cajole. Resistance is protean. It will assume any form, if that's what it takes to deceive you. It will reason with you like a lawyer or jam a nine-millimeter in your face like a stickup man. Resistance has no conscience. It will pledge anything to get a deal, then double-cross you as soon as your back is turned. If you take Resistance at its word, you deserve everything you get. Resistance is always lying and always full of shit.[4]

Thousands of years ago, when saber-toothed tigers and other nasties roamed the land, it might have made sense for humans to be conservative and rule out action unless it was absolutely necessary. But in these modern times, you are unlikely to face life-threatening risks by trying something new. If you want to have a rich and varied life, you can—and should—learn to take action *even though* you are getting warning messages not to.

WHEN YOU RESIST	WHEN YOU TAKE ACTION
You let things pile up so that they become a weight on your shoulders.	You get things done each day so that you are energized by constant progress.
You deny your dreams by pushing them into the future.	You validate your dreams by testing them in the present.
You get lost in trivial tasks.	You spend time on things that matter.
You take your life for granted.	You appreciate the preciousness of each day.
You feel limited by your problems.	You act based on your strengths.
You feel disheartened because your life is on hold.	You wake up excited to do what you enjoy.
You feel hopelessly stuck because nothing ever changes.	You feel light on your feet because each day is full of surprises.
You wait for the big payoff in the future.	You act on your present opportunities.
You postpone things until you are in a better mood.	You get going to change your mood.
You wait for the time to be right.	You leap into it because the time is right.
You hold off trying until you feel confident.	You try things so that your confidence grows.

Don't Trust Your Mystery Moods

*Resistance knows that the more psychic energy we expend dredging
and redredging the tired, boring injustices of our personal lives,
the less juice we have to do our work.*

—STEVEN PRESSFIELD, *THE WAR OF ART: BREAK THROUGH
THE BLOCKS AND WIN YOUR INNER CREATIVE BATTLES*

Laney is a financial analyst employed at the corporate offices of a major life insurance company. Although she is talented at her job, for the last five years she has felt bored with her work. After a long day sitting in front of her computer, she often feels grumpy and impatient. In addition to having a degree in economics, Laney has a master's degree in philosophy and is a dedicated painter. She feels that she would be happier if she could find work with a more creative emphasis, preferably in a diverse and interactive environment.

One day, Laney saw a posting for a job at a local university. The university was seeking a financial director for a new learning initiative within the philosophy department. When Laney first read the job posting, her heart began to race with the excitement. It was exactly what she had been looking for! She was amazed to find that the job qualifications closely matched her background. It was almost like it had been cooked up specifically for her. She decided that she would shape up her résumé and complete an application over the weekend.

When Saturday came, Laney's initial enthusiasm had waned. She tried to sit down and work on her résumé, but she felt unmotivated. She decided to wait for a day when she was more energetic.

The next week at work was quite hectic. Each night when Laney came home, she thought about applying for the job, but she felt too tired. She began to wonder if she really was interested in switching careers. The more she thought about it, the more it began to look like a kooky idea. It had taken years for her to work her way up to her current position, and she suspected that the university job would pay less and require more work. She kept worrying about the job for the next three weeks, until the posting was removed. Laney felt a little guilty for not applying, but she rationalized that since she was never 100 percent enthusiastic, it had probably not been a good job for her.

When an opportunity arose and it came time to act, Laney's resistance stopped her in her tracks. She felt unmotivated and unsure, so she did nothing. Most of us have experienced similar occasions when we let our negative feelings stop us from taking chances. It happens when facing big, potentially life-changing opportunities, as well as simple, day-to-day choices. Do any of the following sound familiar?

- You take a day off from working on your novel (or painting, sculpture, jewelry design) because you aren't feeling passionate enough.
- You get home from work and start to change clothes so you can go to the gym. But then you decide you are too tired, so you sit down and watch TV for the night.
- You begin dating someone new and you instantly click. But after a month, you begin to have a vague sense that things aren't quite right. You take this feeling as a sign that you must not be a good match and call things off.
- You have been eagerly awaiting a new theater performance. The play opens during a busy month at work. You feel like you are probably too stressed out to appreciate the performance, so you skip it.
- A friend working in Europe invites you to come visit her. You are excited by the opportunity and agree to come.

But when you start to think about getting ready for the trip, you feel overwhelmed. You call your friend and tell her that you are too busy—maybe next time.

- You have learned about a neighborhood bridge group. You have been curious about learning bridge for a while, so you plan on attending the group's next meeting. But when the meeting day comes, you don't feel up for socializing with new people, so you stay home.

- You hear about a fascinating training program (East-West medicine, art therapy, conflict resolution, French pastry baking, becoming an inventor, etc.). You are eager to sign up and get started. But then you think about how you will need to commit for the next six weeks, and you worry that this will conflict with other responsibilities. So you take a pass.

We often hear people talk about the importance of trusting their "gut" or "intuition" when deciding what to do. When faced with an opportunity, they will check to see how they feel about it. If they have a good feeling, then they will pursue it; if they have a bad feeling, they will assume that there is some reason—perhaps hidden—as to why moving forward would be undesirable.

Although your immediate feelings can be an important reference point when considering potential courses of action (our approach is based on the importance of trying *fun*, new things), your mood in the moment is not always a reliable indicator of the best way to proceed. The problem is that your neural systems produce a negative emotional response when confronted with unfamiliar situations. This tendency is illustrated by the research of Tanya Chartrand, a psychologist at Duke University.

Chartrand suggests that people tend to repeat patterns of behavior that they have found to work in the past. Over time, these behaviors become unconscious goals. For example, when John, a shy, young man, first begins attending college dorm-room parties, he may carefully monitor how the party provides opportunities for him to mingle with others. Over time, he forms an unconscious goal about how he should act at parties (e.g., sip beer while scanning for dance partners; make funny comments over loud music). If, in later years, he attends a party where he is unable to follow his usual script (e.g., the party features a bingo game with a bunch of teetotalers), he may fall into a funk, even though he won't know why.

Chartrand conducted a variety of studies examining what happens when people succeed or fail at unconscious goals. Her work builds upon previous research into the effects of subconscious stimuli on people's actions. If you briefly show a word to someone viewing a computer monitor, the person will report seeing nothing but a flash of light. But even though the person is unaware of having been shown a word, it will still influence his subsequent behavior. (In psychology this is called "subliminal priming.") People who are briefly shown words related to stereotypical characteristics of the elderly (e.g., forgetful, wrinkled, Florida) will afterward walk more slowly than people who are flashed neutral words (e.g., car, mountain, cup). People who are shown words related to rudeness are more likely to interrupt a later conversation than are people shown words related to politeness.[5]

In one study led by Chartrand, participants were subliminally flashed words related to personal characteristics (e.g., opinion, personality) in order to give them the unconscious goal of forming impressions of people. A control group was presented with neutral words. Next, the participants were presented with a person's description that included inconsistent traits (e.g., clumsy and agile), making it difficult for them to form a coherent impression. Participants who had been primed to form an impression reported a more negative mood than the control group, even though they couldn't identify the reason for their dimmed spirits. Chatrand calls such negative feelings that arise when unconscious goals go unmet "mystery moods," because people don't know why they are experiencing them.

We like the phrase "mystery moods" because it helps debunk the unwarranted authority that so many people bestow upon their negative feelings. If someone asks you why you decided not to pursue a job possibility, it sounds a lot better to say "I had a bad feeling about it and I decided to trust my intuition" than it does to say "I decided not to do anything because my mystery mood wasn't chipper enough."

The negative feelings that arise in the face of change and uncertainty can be quite convincing. They say that you are too frightened, exhausted, embarrassed, anxious, sad, doubtful, or uninterested to do anything. They declare themselves to be unshakable and enduring ("You are *always* going to feel too scared to take the MCAT"), and assert that it is hopeless to try to act against them. This brings to mind the wonderful movie *The Wizard of Oz*. The wizard appears frightening and all-powerful, but when the curtain is pulled back, he is found to be a harmless old man. Your moods are the same. The way you pull back the curtain to uncloak them is by taking action *despite* feeling like you can't or shouldn't.

Move Your Mood

The best way to get in the mood to do something is by doing it. Suppose you decide to change your evening routine by going for an evening walk instead of sitting down at your computer and surfing the web. When

Move Your Mood

The next time you are about to talk yourself out of doing something because you aren't feeling up to the task, do it anyway to change how you feel. Say to yourself, "I'm going to ____ so that I can get in the mood for it." For example:

- If you are feeling too lethargic to exercise, go to the gym so that you feel more energetic.
- If you are nervous about approaching potential clients for your new consulting business, go talk to potential clients so that you develop greater confidence.
- If you are feeling uninspired to work on the book you are writing, sit down and start typing so that your creativity can start to flow.
- If you feel overwhelmed by the prospect of applying for a new job, spend five minutes sprucing up your résumé so that you are more excited about career possibilities.
- If you are feeling too stressed out to enjoy socializing, chat on the phone with a friend so that you feel appreciative of others.
- If you are feeling overwhelmed by a complicated project, sit down and spend a few minutes working on one of its easier components. This will make the project feel more manageable and build your confidence in your ability to tackle it.

you come home from work, you are likely to feel tired and want to plop down in front of your computer as usual. But if you get yourself to step outside and start walking, after a few minutes, you will begin to enjoy it.

Not only is taking action the fastest way to establish a more positive attitude toward doing something, it is also often the *only* way you can come to feel positive and comfortable about unfamiliar activities. Consider public speaking. No matter how much you prepare and try to psych yourself up in advance, you are probably going to feel anxious the first few times you give a presentation in front of an audience. If your plan is to wait until you feel comfortable before you speak publicly, you will never do it. The same holds true for facing new social settings, occupations, creative projects, and relationships. If you wait until you are free of anxiety and doubt, then you are going to spend a lot of time doing nothing.

The truth is that how you feel has little to do with your ability to take positive action. We routinely do incredible things despite not feeling gung ho about them. We learn to walk and talk. Women give birth. We stay up for days caring for our ill children. We get up and go to work each day. Our powers to act in the face of adversity far outstrip our wimpy moods. So don't let your temporary negative feelings stop you from taking chances and trying new things. Feeling fear is often a good thing—a sign that you are moving into uncharted territories that will stretch you and bring personal growth.

Walk Through the Malodorous Middle

Every project has its highs and lows, and many—especially those entailing creativity and uncertainty—have what we call the *malodorous middle*, the time when progress slows, enthusiasm wanes, and success feels unlikely. Tim Brown, the CEO of the iconic design company IDEO, is intimately familiar with the way that projects bog down in the middle. He says that design is "rarely a graceful leap from height to height." New projects usually begin with enthusiasm and optimism. But then comes the tough middle part where designers grapple with conflicting objectives and face the daunting challenge of integrating a hodgepodge of ideas into a fresh design. During this time, it is common to get discouraged.

The designers at IDEO have learned that if they persist despite their doubt, they will eventually begin to make small gains, which over time build in momentum and lead to an exciting new design. One of the designers drew a "project mood chart" to illustrate the different emotional phases of product design. The chart has a U-shaped curve that begins with a peak labeled "hope," corresponding to the giddy early days of a project. Then comes a negative valley labeled "insight," the depressing time when designers chug away with seemingly little progress. This is followed by another positive peak labeled "confidence," when ideas cohere into a design solution.

The malodorous middle is a time when we are particularly vulnerable to resistance. When forward progress on a project slows and the path to completion is unclear, your negative mood may make you think that you have permanently lost your joy, that your project was a misguided idea, or that you don't have the necessary aptitude or skills to finish.

What do you do when you have to cross a stinky room? You hold your nose and keep walking. Similarly, when you find yourself in the malodorous middle of a project, the best thing to do is to keep chipping away at the task in front of you. By doing so, you will often find that your enthusiasm and creative juices kick in again.

We should note that we are not advocating sticking rigidly to every plan. It is often appropriate to change course—sometimes radically. An easy way to recognize if you are being stopped by a temporary negative feeling, as opposed to an authentic need for change, is to see what happens when you get engaged in your work. If you start working and find that your interest and energy return, then it is likely that you have been beset by a temporary mood. At such times, it is best to just keep plugging away.

Build Your Grit

If you want to be successful, then you need to have old-fashioned stick-to-itiveness, or what Penn psychologist Angela Duckworth calls "grit." Duckworth studies leaders in the fields of investment banking, painting, journalism, academia, medicine, and law to determine why some people accomplish significantly more than others with similar intelligence, creativity, and talent.[6] Her research shows that leaders in most fields share one essential characteristic: grit.

> We define grit as perseverance and passion for long-term goals. Grit entails working strenuously toward challenges, maintaining effort and interest over years despite failure, adversity, and plateaus in progress. The gritty individual approaches achievement as a marathon; his or her advantage is stamina. Whereas disappointment or boredom signals to others that it is time to change trajectory and cut losses, the gritty individual stays the course.

The importance of perseverance in personal achievement has been illustrated by the work of educational psychologist Benjamin Bloom, who made substantial contributions to the understanding of mastery-learning. In a study of the development of world-class pianists, chess players, sculptors, neurologists, and swimmers, Bloom found that sheer talent alone was not enough for mastery. In fact, only a few of the high achievers included in the study were considered prodigies by their teachers. The three general characteristics that Bloom found to characterize world-class performers were a passion for their field, a desire to reach "a high level of attainment," and a "willingness to put in great amounts of time and effort."[7]

The research of Duckworth and Bloom is encouraging in that it shows that personal achievement is not just a matter of your innate talent, but is, more important, a result of *what you do*. Research has also shown that grit can build over time. A group of Australian researchers recently completed a study that measured the impact of a two-month exercise program on the self-regulation of twenty-four students.[8] The participants were given psychological tests every two weeks and kept daily journals of their behaviors. Those that participated in the exercise group reported a range of positive benefits related to enhanced self-control. They smoked less, consumed less alcohol and caffeine, ate less junk food, reduced their impulse shopping, and procrastinated less. The researchers characterized self-regulations as a renewable resource that could be depleted as well as recharged over time. It appears that grit is like a muscle; the more you use it, the stronger it gets.

Although we can't predict what path your life will take, we can guarantee that you will be more happy and successful if you learn to stick with the things that are most important to you.

Overcome Procrastination

Things may come to those who wait,
but only the things left by those who hustle.

—ABRAHAM LINCOLN

There was once an assistant professor of philosophy at a top university who was struggling to finish his first book, the success of which would determine whether he would attain tenure. The professor was besieged with academic responsibilities—teaching, faculty meetings, student supervision, reviewing journal articles, participating in conferences—and found it difficult to carve out time to think deeply and write. He also felt pressured by the expectations of his department. He was considered one of the rising stars on the faculty, and his colleagues were awaiting a landmark book, not merely a good one. Taken together, these factors put the young professor in a state of paralysis. He couldn't write a single paragraph.

To try to break out of his writing funk, the professor sought professional help. He met with a Freudian analyst who, after a year of sessions, revealed that the professor resisted academic success due to a deep-seated fear of distancing himself from his blue-collar father. The following year, the professor began to meet with a cognitive psychologist, who found that the professor needed to overcome self-limiting thinking styles.

Despite the help from these experts, the professor remained stuck in writing paralysis for five years. Although he was still not making progress on his book, he at least felt justified in his inactivity. How could he be expected to tackle such a huge project when he was such a mess? It was in this frame of mind that he met with a new counselor.

During their first session, the professor described the many obstacles he faced in completing his book—his emotional issues, negative cognitive patterns, the heroic intellectual challenge of the project, and the stupendous pressure that the book be a success. After speaking for about thirty minutes, the professor settled back in his chair, feeling a little proud of his lucid summation of his predicament. The counselor sat a long time, deep in thought. Then he spoke. "There's nothing I can do for you," he said. "You just need to go and write."

The professor was taken aback. He had been looking forward to a stimulating discourse about psychology, philosophy, and the rigors of academic life. But for some reason, the forceful directness of the therapist's words had an impact. So the professor went home, took out his typewriter (this was before the advent of word processors), and began to tap away. He wrote for twenty minutes that first day. The next morning, he woke up and wrote some more. Within a few days, he was immersed in the project. He worked relentlessly and finished the book in the next six months. When it was published, the book was met with great acclaim. The professor was granted tenure and became a leader in the field.

So what happened? What changed that allowed the professor to finally get going and write his book? He didn't resolve his emotional problems, improve his thinking, or come up with better ways to manage his anxiety. What changed is that instead of fretting about writing, he just started doing it. Despite his worries and concerns, he sat down at his desk and started typing.

Like the professor, many of us are great procrastinators. We know that we have important work we should do—projects to complete, books to write, résumés to submit, taxes to file, potential customers to approach, new curiosities to explore—but we just can't bring ourselves to get going. Time and time again we come up with action plans, resolutions, and to-do lists. Then, feeling uplifted by our fresh commitment to action, we decide to take the day off.

Procrastination is the most tricky (and familiar) way that resistance discourages us from action. Instead of directly trying to talk us out of doing something, it just suggests that we postpone things for a better day. "Don't worry," it will say, "you are going to get going like gangbusters writing that novel. But let's go for a walk today while the sun is out." Procrastination is the hidden killer of dreams.

Develop the Do-It-Today Habit

Most of us have busy lives, and there is no shortage of tasks to do. Our resistance loves to remind us of our various obligations in order to keep us from actions that might shake up the status quo. It will say, "Working on your dissertation is important, but wouldn't it be best to go buy groceries before the store gets crowded?" Or "You're going to jump right into finishing that website for your business—right after you read your email." Or "It would be wonderful to try that class on rock climbing; but it can wait until you finish that financial report for work."

Procrastination is complex and can take many different forms. But as intricate and convoluted as our reasons for our procrastination can be, the solution boils down to something pretty simple: *Spend time every day working on your most important projects.*

In his book *The Now Habit: A Strategic Program for Overcoming Procrastination and Enjoying Guilt-Free Play*, the psychologist Neil Fiore presents a process for combating procrastination, which he calls the "unschedule."[9] The idea is that instead of worrying about sticking to an overall plan for a project, you strive to complete thirty minutes of work:

> Think small. Do not aim to finish a book, write letters, complete
> your income tax, or to work continuously for even four hours.
> Aim for thirty minutes of quality, focused work.

The key point is to get in the habit of doing *quality* work that isn't interrupted by checking your email, surfing the web, or trips to the refrigerator. By doing thirty minutes of focused work, you overcome your inertia and reignite your interest. This helps change your mind-set from being a procrastinator to being a producer.

Most of us are amazingly inventive at coming up with reasons to avoid doing what matters. (It's too bad that procrastination isn't a useful skill!) The antidote to procrastination is to reverse this process—to become skilled at spending time each day engaged in your most significant work. It can be helpful to create a list of key activities related to your important projects. For example, suppose you are creating a workshop on green business practices and exploring the possibility of becoming a consultant in the field. Your list of key activities might include:

- Write on the subject of green business practices
- Read books, blogs, and research articles on the subject of green business practices
- Help educate others about green business practices
- Learn something new about green business operations
- Talk to experts in the field of green business practices
- Come up with new ideas about promoting green business practices
- Invent new green business practices
- Ask questions about green business practices
- Establish friendships with people involved in the field of green business practices
- File new information on green business practices
- Speak with production line employees, business owners, and corporate managers on the subject of green business practices
- Discover new resources related to green business practices

Once you have created a list of tasks, get in the habit of engaging in at least one of them every day. Don't worry about how much time you spend working—it can be as little as a few minutes. Returning to our example, you could read a page in a related book or file a single document. *The crucial thing is that you engage in at least one of your key tasks each day.*

When you spend time each day engaged in work that matters to you, you improve your mood, build momentum, stir up your creativity, and become attuned to the opportunities around you. So don't wait—get to work on something important today.

Turn Someday into Today

If you are like most people, you probably have a list of tasks that you have been wanting to get around to—home-improvement projects, fitness goals, creative work, business development—but haven't yet found the time or motivation to get started. Make a list of these things that you want to do, and come up with a way you can get going today. Here are some examples:

ONE DAY	TODAY
I will lose weight.	I will eat a light lunch.
I will improve employee morale.	I will take Cindy to lunch to reward her fine work.
I will get out of debt.	I will save one dollar to pay off my credit card.
I will get in shape.	I will go for a walk after work.
I will improve my relationship.	I will buy a card to show my love.
I will write a children's book.	I will write a few sentences on the bus ride home.
I will reconnect with my friends.	I will call my friend Steve.
I will pursue my business idea.	I will chat with an expert to explore my idea.

Have you created your list? Great! Now start doing something!

9

It Takes a Community

. . . .

*What a person does on his own, without being stimulated
by the thoughts and experiences of others, is even in the
best of cases rather paltry and monotonous.*

—ALBERT EINSTEIN

*It is hardly possible to overrate the value . . . of placing human
beings in contact with persons dissimilar to themselves, and with
modes of thought and action unlike those with which they are
familiar . . . Such communication has always been, and is
peculiarly in the present age, one of the primary sources of progress.*

—JOHN STUART MILL

*World-class professionals build networks to help them navigate the
world. No matter how brilliant your mind or strategy, if you're
playing a solo game, you'll always lose out to a team. Athletes
need coaches and trainers, child prodigies need parents and teachers,
directors need producers and actors, politicians need donors and
strategists, scientists need lab partners and mentors. Penn needed
Teller. Ben needed Jerry. Steve Jobs needed Steve Wozniak.
Indeed, teamwork is eminently on display in the start-up world.*

*Very few start-ups are started by one person. Everyone in
the entrepreneurial community agrees that assembling
a talented team is as important as it gets.*

—LINKEDIN FOUNDER REID HOFFMAN AND COAUTHOR BEN
CASNOCHA IN THEIR BOOK, *THE START-UP OF YOU*[1]

IF YOU STUDY the lives of successful people, you will find that
most every story of personal success is founded upon the help and
support of friends, mentors, advisors, and family. You will also find
that many of the most transformative experiences and opportunities
that people encounter come as the result of their social interactions.
It is hard to conceive of a definition of personal success that does not
include a supportive community.

We use the word "community" rather than the word "networking" because we want to suggest a different way to think about
personal relationships. Traditional business networking, with its focus on seeking people who can provide resources that you need—
sales leads, business referrals, professional introductions—can feel
cold and artificial. People recognize when you are interacting with
them as a means to get something and will rightfully be wary of you.
In contrast, when your goal is to build a community, you *commune*
with others; you converse intimately in order to share the fullness of
your humanity—mutual joy, enthusiasm, curiosity, values, feelings,
whimsy, and aspirations.

*There is no more powerful way to enrich your life and encounter the
unknown than by having meaningful relationships with a wide range of
people.* In this chapter, we will present twelve simple steps you can
take to reach out to new people and strengthen your ties with those
whom you already know.

Surround Yourself with Role Models

Keep away from people who try to belittle your ambitions.
Small people always do that, but the really great make you
feel that you, too, can become great.

—MARK TWAIN

Over fifty years ago, Swarthmore College researcher Solomon Asch devised an ingenious experiment to show the impact of social influence.[2] College students were asked to perform what was called a simple "vision test." The real point of the study was not to test visual acuity but to explore how social conformity impacts people's behavior.

Each student was placed in a group with five to seven confederates who knew the aims of the study but who the student thought were other students taking the test. The group members were presented a card with a line on it and a second card with three lines, and were asked to choose which of the lines on the second card (A, B, or C) was of the same length as the line on the first card.

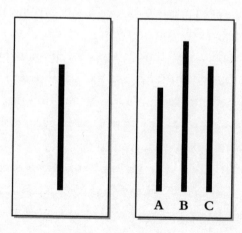

A   B   C

The real study participants were asked to provide their answers after the confederates gave their response. When the confederates first selected the correct line (C), only one out of thirty-five participants gave an incorrect response. But when the confederates selected the wrong line (B), the study participants gave an incorrect answer 32 percent of the time; 75 percent of them gave at least one incorrect response.

In a follow-up experiment, the confederate responses were varied to see how unanimity impacted social conformity.[3] If one confederate dissented from the others and provided a correct response, then far fewer study participants (5–10 percent) provided an incorrect response.

Asch's experiments show how the people around you shape the actions that you take. They also illustrated the importance of allies. Just one person who supports your view can provide you the courage to stick to your guns and act appropriately.

In a more recent study led by Dr. Nicholas Christakis of Harvard Medical School, 12,067 people were followed over a span of thirty-two years to examine the impact of social influence on obesity.[4] Remarkably, the study found that obesity is contagious: If one of your close mutual friends becomes obese, it increases the chances that you will become obese by 57 percent. More amazing, if a friend of your friend becomes obese—even one who lives in a different city—this will still increase the likelihood of your becoming obese by 25 percent. In summarizing his findings, Dr. Christakis said, "You change your idea of what is an acceptable body type by looking at the people around you."

In Dr. Christakis's fascinating book *Connected: The Surprising Power of Our Social Networks and How They Shape Our Lives*, written with coauthor James Fowler, a wide range of studies are reviewed, highlighting the many ways that people influence and copy one another.[5] Homeowners who have neighbors with tidy yards tend to have meticulous lawns. Students with studious roommates hit the books more. Diners seated next to heavy eaters consume more food. People with upbeat friends are happier. Depression, suicide, violence, and loneliness are similarly "contagious"—or flow from one person to the next.

Research into social influence shows that the people in your life influence both what you do and what you perceive to be possible. Behaviors and ideas are contagious: If you surround yourself with dynamic, enthusiastic people, then you will be positive and proactive as well.

Diversify Your Community

In their book *The Innovator's DNA: Mastering the Five Skills of Disruptive Innovators*, Jeff Dyer and his coauthors discuss the difference between networking for resources and networking for ideas.[6] In the typical approach to networking, individuals form relationships with similar people in order to attain resources—business contacts, sales leads, investors. Successful innovators have a different approach to social relationships. They deliberately seek out people with backgrounds and perspectives different from their own so that they can extend their knowledge. Dyer and his colleagues call this form of networking *idea networking*:

> The basic principle of idea networking—as opposed to resource networking—is to build a bridge into a different area of knowledge by interacting with someone with whom you, or people within your primary social networks, typically do not interact.[7]

The researchers note that idea-networking often leads to serendipity. Entrepreneurs often stumble upon key ideas and opportunities when interacting with people outside their usual social circle. In about half of the business cases they studied where entrepreneurs formed new ideas as a result of social interactions, the lucky individuals came upon the new idea by chance. As an example, they discuss the story of Joe Morton, who came up with a billion-dollar idea when traveling in Malaysia.[8]

Morton lived in Malaysia for a year and heard many Malaysians talking about the health benefits of the fruit mangosteen. Morton tried mangosteen and found it to be delicious. He contacted his brother, David, who was getting his Ph.D. at the University of Utah Medical School, and asked him to see if there were any research studies that examined the health benefits of mangosteen. David found that there were numerous studies indicating the fruit's beneficial characteristics. This led Morton in 2002 to found XANGO, a company that sells mangosteen juice. In just six years, XANGO grew to be a billion-dollar company.

Morton would not have come up with the idea for his company if he had not talked to the locals in Malaysia and been exposed to information that was unavailable to his contacts back home. The research of the University of Chicago sociologist Ron Burt has shown that inventive ideas often arise from interacting with people outside of one's social norm. Business managers with access to broad social networks earn higher salaries, have better performance reviews, and receive more frequent promotions than managers without such extensive connections.

People connected to groups beyond their own can expect to find themselves delivering valuable ideas, seeming to be gifted with creativity. This is not creativity born of genius; it is creativity as an import-export business. An idea mundane in one group can be a valuable insight in another.[9]

Burt's description of creativity as a function of information exchange, rather than an act of individual genius, matches our experience working with our clients. Oftentimes, the insight or idea that proves transformative arises from seemingly chance social encounters. The story of how Sheila started her business provides a nice example of this.

Working with the Dogs

Sheila was a talented young architect working for a northern California corporation. The work environment was stressful and competitive, with a handful of associates vying for a few prized partnership positions. Sheila hated the long hours, cutthroat atmosphere, and incessant focus on the bottom line. She dreamed of opening a boutique architecture firm, the kind of place where you could bring your dog to work, be surrounded by collaborative colleagues, and have the freedom to take on projects that were interesting design problems, not just proven moneymakers.

The problem with Sheila's dream was that the architecture industry is extremely competitive. Unless you can differentiate yourself by becoming an expert in a niche, it is very hard to build an independent practice. Sheila spent about a year mulling over ideas for her own company. She looked into specializing in historical renovations, as well as designing schools, but she found that there were many well-established firms fighting for this work.

Feeling stuck and out of options, Sheila came to see Ryan to get help moving forward with her plans. She told Ryan that she felt like she was trapped in "corporate hell." Her present work was so stressful and unfulfilling that she was beginning to doubt whether she should have ever become an architect.

Ryan asked Sheila about her aspirations, and she shared her dream of opening her own firm. She talked about the different areas of specialty she had explored, and how frustrating it was that none of them had panned out. Ryan noted that Sheila didn't appear to lack motivation or ideas, but she did seem to be in need of a fresh perspective. He encouraged her to begin to talk to a wider community of people to explore ways she could form her own company.

At first, Sheila was hesitant to approach people, as she thought that it would make her look flaky to be asking for career advice. She also worried that people would be too busy to meet with her, especially given that there was little that they had to gain from the conversation. But she was happily surprised to find that many people were willing to meet with her for lunch or coffee and give her helpful advice and encouragement. As Sheila began to talk to different people in the building industry, she saw that there were many pathways to starting one's own company. This helped her to feel more positive and patient about her current work situation. She saw that she wasn't trapped but was actively moving herself toward the right opportunity.

During this time of exploration, Sheila got a surprise call from an old college friend who asked if she would like to meet. In the past, Sheila was so busy and stressed out by work that she probably would have turned down this invitation. But given that she was already in the process of reaching out to people, Sheila agreed to meet her friend for lunch.

It turned out that Sheila's friend was a commercial business broker who was trying to close a deal on a building in downtown Berkeley. The potential buyer—let's call him Tom—was hoping to use the building for a medical clinic. A tentative purchase offer had been made on the building and accepted, but at the last hour, Tom found out that four hundred feet of building space was taken up by a hallway and staircase, and therefore unavailable for general use. Thinking that the reduced space would make it impossible for him to create the type of clinic he had envisioned, Tom now wanted to walk away from the deal.

When Shelia heard about her friend's problem, a little lightbulb went off in her head. She mentioned how she was an architect who was looking into branching out, and said that she would be happy to meet with Tom free of charge to look over the space to see if it could be made to meet his needs. Her friend passed this information on to Tom, and he agreed—albeit somewhat reluctantly—to talk to Sheila.

Sheila met Tom at the building, which was a 1950s structure in a mixed-use community. Tom began to discuss the needs for the clinic—a waiting room that could accommodate twenty people, six examination rooms, a lab, a stockroom, and so on. As they toured the interior, Sheila pointed out how areas of the building could be altered to open up the workspace and allow more natural light. She also noted that there was a wall at a rear storage area that could be removed to add floor space.

After meeting with Sheila, Tom felt confident that the building would meet his needs, so he resubmitted his purchase offer and it was accepted. He was so impressed by Sheila's ideas that he hired her to design the layout for the clinic. Sheila worked during the evening and weekends to come up with the plans. She had never thought of designing a medical clinic—she admitted that if she had, she probably would have guessed it to be boring—but she found the work to be interesting and challenging. When she completed the project, Tom referred her to another friend who needed help designing a dental clinic. Sheila excitedly accepted the project, and two months later gave notice at her job. She had found her niche!

Fast-forward three years, Sheila has now built a small, thriving architecture practice designing medical clinics. Most recently, she designed a series of centers for a national nonprofit agency promoting community health. She has hired an assistant architect as well as a part-time project manager. All three of them are dog owners, and the dogs—a beagle, Lab, and bearded collie—strut around the office as if they own the place. With all the costs of running her own company, Sheila is making slightly less money than she did as an associate at her old firm. But she is quite happy to trade a little income in the short term for building her own business and working in a fun, friendly environment. As she puts it, it is better to work *with* the dogs than it is to work *like* a dog.

How Diverse Is Your Community?

In childhood and early adulthood, most of us interact with a wide variety of people. But as we age and become more settled in our lives, we spend more of our time with people who are like us—who live in the same neighborhood, are about the same age, and have similar jobs, income, and life orientation. Take a moment to consider the diversity of your social relationships. Of the people you know, how many are:

- Children, teenagers, young adults, middle-aged, elderly?
- Employed in the arts, media, entertainment, health, engineering, construction, academia, high tech, government, manufacturing, small business, church?
- Come from the United States, Eastern Europe, Africa, Southeast Asia?
- Live in a rural setting, cosmopolitan apartment, foreign country, international community?

- Are wealthy, middle class, working class, or poor?
- Are oriented toward creativity, business, exploring the world, improving communities, pursuing wisdom, advancing technology, accumulating money, mentoring the young, mastering a sport?

If your social community isn't very diverse, you can dramatically open up the possibilities in your life by getting to know people who are different from those with whom you normally associate.

Meet a New Person Each Week

A simple way to expand your social relationships is to talk to a new person each week. Strike up a conversation with a stranger, get to know a new person at work, or have coffee with a neighbor or member of your church group. Don't worry about whether this interaction leads to a long-term friendship. The point is to enjoy meeting someone new and to learn about his or her life experience. It is a bit like stopping to appreciate the beauty of a flower. Be curious, appreciative, and open to being surprised. And make sure the person knows that you value his or her perspective.

Sustain Contact

Over the course of your life, you have probably established friendships with many different people. But amid the busyness of your life, you may find that you don't spend the necessary time sustaining your relationships. How many dear friends do you have that you have lost touch with, or whom you speak with only once a year?

One of the easiest ways to broaden your social community is to reach out to those whom you already know. Every week, call someone to touch base and say hello, meet with an old friend over a meal, or contact a school mate or work colleague from the past. Once you get in the habit of doing this, you will find it takes much less effort than you imagined, and it will contribute substantially to your life. Is it uncomfortable to change your past habits? Yes—but do it anyway.

Form a Mastermind Group

When you are considering an opportunity, negotiating a complex problem, or trying to generate new ideas, it can be helpful to seek out the advice of a friend or colleague who can provide a different perspective. You can deliberately put this process to work by creating what in the coaching world is called a *Mastermind Group*, three to six people who meet regularly to brainstorm and support one another. Many extraordinary people are known for forming such groups. Ben Franklin, along with twelve of his most ingenious friends in Philadelphia, formed a group dedicated to self-improvement that met weekly to share books and ideas.[10] Henry Ford formed a group of close advisors that included the inventor Thomas Edison and the management genius Harvey Firestone. More recently, Richard Branson, when he founded Virgin Music, created an idea-sharing group composed of producers, musicians, artists, and filmmakers.

There are a few things to keep in mind when forming a Mastermind Group. First, you should include people with diverse backgrounds, skill sets, and talents. The group should ideally include between four and six people. If you have fewer than three people, then your group may suffer from insufficient diversity and interactive dynamics, and if you have more than six, it may not provide enough opportunity for each member to discuss his or her views and concerns. The group should meet on a regular basis—for example, biweekly or monthly. Ideally, the meetings should occur in person, although effective groups can also meet by phone. During the meeting, each member should be given an allocation of time to describe what he or she is working on and thinking about, and allow others to provide comments and suggestions.

In addition to providing a diversity of views and perspectives, an advantage of forming a Mastermind Group is that it keeps its members accountable. At each meeting, participants can describe the actions they will take and set deadlines to complete them. In doing so, they will be held accountable to those commitments. This can be quite helpful in encouraging you to take positive actions that are in alignment with your highest priorities.

Become a Teacher

A great way to meet new people and form deep friendships is by becoming a teacher. There are many ways you can do this. You can tutor high school students, teach an introductory class at a club you belong to, lead a brown-bag discussion at work, or help coach a children's sports team. When you share your expertise, it provides a valuable opportunity to reflect upon your own experience, as well as to learn about the lives of others. You will also benefit from the satisfaction that comes from helping others to learn and grow.

Interview an Expert

Another way to meet new people and broaden your experience is to interview an expert in an area you are curious about. For example, if you are interested in making a career change to begin working as a product designer, you can find an established designer whose work you like and ask her if she would be willing to meet for coffee to talk about her experience. People will be more likely to agree to meet with you if you share a little about your background and say what it is about their work and ideas that inspires you. Keep in mind that relationships are never a one-way street. Look for ways to contribute something in return for the expert taking the time to meet with you, whether it is heartfelt thanks or an idea that you might have related to her work.

This brings to mind a conversation that John had with a young woman who sought his advice on exploring new career options. John told her some of the key aspects to his approach—for example, that you don't need to make a master plan or decide upon a career in advance. The woman was moved by this conversation and wrote a thank-you message in which she listed John's ideas that she found most helpful. She wrote about John's approach to counseling in her blog, and because of this, six individuals have contacted John to share ideas.

Attend a Conference, Workshop, or Class

Attending conferences, workshops, and classes provides a great way to be introduced to new ideas and meet a wide variety of people.

You can attend events that are related to your current area of work or expertise, as well as those that cover subjects that are new to you. When attending a conference or class, make a point to get to know the other attendees and learn about their backgrounds, what they study, experts they follow, books they read, ideas they are excited about, and what suggestions they might have regarding your own aspirations and problems. If you have a friendly conversation, make sure that you get their contact information and have a business card to hand out with your own contact information.

Set Up a Mealtime or Tea-Time Social Schedule

Mealtimes and coffee breaks can provide a convenient time to meet with new people or strengthen your existing relationships. For example, you might set aside Friday lunch as a time to meet with a new person each week, and Sunday dinner as a time to catch up with old friends.

Get Introductions (and Provide Them)

When you meet with someone with whom you have a good rapport, the following is a good question to ask (or some variation of it): "Whom do you know who might be good for me to talk to?" Even if you feel a little uncomfortable asking this question, you should do so anyway—the rewards can be huge. There are many people out there who might become friends or professional allies, but you will never get to meet them unless you are introduced by someone they

know. Successful people realize the importance of personal introductions and will happily provide them, as long as you ask in a
matter-of-fact way.

You should also get in the habit of providing introductions when
you feel that they will be beneficial to the people involved. It is a
simple thing for you to do, but it can be tremendously helpful to
others.

Join a Club or Community Group

Clubs and community groups are other places you can easily meet
new people. So you might want to try to attend one group a month.
To keep things interesting, you can attend groups that are oriented
toward topics that intrigue you, as well as those that have a focus that
is entirely new to you.

If you are having trouble finding interesting groups, you might
want to check out the website www.meetup.com. This company
makes it easy to create interest groups—for hiking, art, cooking,
philosophy, whatever. If you search in your area, you are likely to
find groups focused on some of your favorite topics. If a group
doesn't exist, then you can create your own.

Follow Through

Have you ever met someone you liked but didn't bother to give him
a call? Have you been invited to a party but chosen to stay at home?
A simple way to enrich your social life is by following through. If
you meet someone whom you would like to get to know, resist your
inertia and set up a time to meet. When you are invited to a social

occasion, make the effort to show up and enjoy the people who are there. When someone helps you, take the time to write a thank-you message.

Tips for Introverts

The authors of this book, both being introverts, understand that it is not always easy to approach new people. But we have found that the rewards that come from our relationships far outweigh the discomfort we might feel when interacting with unfamiliar people. Here are a few tips that we have found to be helpful:

1. *Have low expectations.* Because introverts find interactions with unknown people to be stressful, they often avoid attending social events unless they are certain that the event will be fun and rewarding. For example, you might be invited to a party and decide not to go because you don't think you have enough in common with the people who will be there. The truth is that social occasions often fall short of being scintillating, but they may still provide the opportunity to meet new people and to be introduced to new ideas. So don't set high expectations when considering attending an event. Just ask yourself, "Is there a chance I will have a pleasant conversation or two?" If so, go.

2. *Never make a cold call.* Calling people out of the blue can feel awkward and uncomfortable. You can lessen this discomfort by finding points of commonality between yourself and the person you are contacting. You can almost always find something that you have in common. You may work in the same industry, know the same people, attend the same conferences, belong to the same health club, or have kids in the same elementary school. If you know little about a person's personal life,

you can mention his or her work and how it inspires or intrigues you. Mentioning a shared experience or interest encourages the person to whom you are reaching out to be more relaxed and responsive.

3. *Don't give up.* Our clients often ask us how many times they can contact someone to meet before they will be considered a pest. A good rule of thumb is to ask to meet *at least* three times, each time in a different way. For example, you might call once on the phone, follow up with an email, then send a note in the mail. Remember, successful people are usually busy. Just because they don't respond right away doesn't mean that they aren't interested in meeting with you. The only way to know for sure that someone doesn't want to meet with you is if he tells you no.

4. *Dealing with rejection.* What if you approach someone and she doesn't want to talk to you? The answer is, you pat yourself on the back for trying and move on. The quickest way to get over the sting of rejection is to not let it stop you. There are a multitude of interesting, helpful people out there to meet and get to know.

5. *It's OK to say no.* Some people worry that if they meet someone and don't hit it off, then they will be obligated to continue that relationship. Similarly, they might feel that if they attend a group event that they don't enjoy, then it will look bad if they don't attend again. Don't worry—it is OK to say "no" if you don't feel like continuing your relationship. Trust yourself to not get sucked into something that you don't want to do. It can be helpful to practice some different ways to politely but firmly say no. For example, "I wish I had the time, but I really don't."

6. *It's all about practice.* The more you get in the habit of meeting new people, attending social events, and asking for introductions, the better you will get at it and the less awkward it will be. Also, if you are involved in many different social activities, it lessens the expectations (and worries) related to any particular one.

7. *Just be yourself.* Give yourself a break—you don't always have to be glib, full of jokes, and the life of the party. You just have to be yourself. It is more important to enjoy other people than it is to impress or entertain them. Instead of trying to be more interesting, learn how to appreciate others—admire their strengths, enjoy their stories, and learn from their life experiences.

Afterword: Fail More to Live More

....

We wrote this book with the hope that it would help people lead more fulfilling lives—to boldly pursue what they enjoy, to passionately engage in meaningful work, and to embrace new experiences and the unknown. The Fail Fast approach provides a simple way to transform your life through small, immediate actions. When you embrace failure rather than resist it, every moment provides the opportunity to:

- Learn
- Experience
- Wonder
- Grow
- Get involved
- Create
- Appreciate
- Be surprised
- Share
- Feel connected

We hope you take the message of this book to heart and have fun failing. The more you fail, the more you will live, and you deserve a wonderful life! To help you get started failing as quickly and frequently as possible, we would like to touch upon some of the key ideas presented and provide suggestions as to how you can apply them, beginning today.

Remember the Fun Factor

Throughout this book we have stressed the importance of building enjoyment into your life. By doing what you love, you place yourself in an appreciative mind-set that allows you to think more creatively, work more productively, and capitalize on unexpected opportunities. So starting today, set aside at least five minutes for unadulterated pleasure. Read an interesting book, get a massage, eat a delightful lunch, chat up a friend, or enjoy one of your hobbies.

Do It Badly as Fast as You Can

Successful people have a knack for performing poorly. They deliberately seek out opportunities where they can face the limits of their skills and knowledge so that they can encounter the unknown and learn. In this spirit, we encourage you to find something that you have been meaning to do and to give yourself permission to do it badly right away. For example, you can shake your booty on the dance floor, talk to a sommelier using your rusty college French, or give a presentation at a company event.

Break from Your Routine

You are more likely to encounter unexpected opportunities and ideas when you are doing new things—trying activities, exploring unfamiliar places, meeting people, or being exposed to different ideas or cultures. So find a way today to step out of your usual haunts, habits, and thinking patterns to experience new possibilities. For example, you might drive a different route home from work, introduce yourself to a stranger, attend an offbeat play, or read an unfamiliar magazine.

Un-Plan It

Successful people have a lean approach to planning. They find ways to take small steps in order to experiment, collect information, and adjust course, without the need for a huge investment or long-term commitment. With this in mind, rather than worry about your plans for the next month or year, focus on what you can do *today*. Take a small, immediate step related to your interests or aspirations. For example, you might talk to an expert, visit a company, sign up for a conference, buy a book, or begin building a prototype.

Do It Anyway

It is natural to feel uncertain, unmotivated, or fearful when facing new challenges. But negative feelings shouldn't stop you. The best way to gain confidence and improve your mood is to take action, even though you're not feeling up to it. The next time you find yourself hesitating due to your negative mood, get going anyway. Go for a run even though you feel lethargic; invite a colleague to lunch even though you feel shy; volunteer for a project even though you doubt your abilities; or enroll in a challenging course even though you feel unprepared.

Now it's time for you to get out there and fail as quickly as you possibly can. And then fail again.

Notes

....

CHAPTER 1: THE HAPPINESS TIPPING POINT

1 A. M. Isen. "Positive Affect, Cognitive Processes and Social Behavior." *Advances in Experimental Social Psychology* 20 (1987): 203–253.

2 T. Amabile and S. Kramer. *The Progress Principle: Using Small Wins to Ignite Joy, Engagement, and Creativity at Work* (Cambridge, MA: Harvard Business Review Press, 2011), 56.

3 Ibid., 51.

4 B. L. Fredrickson and C. Branigan. "Positive Emotions Broaden the Scope of Attention and Thought-Action Repertoires," *Cognition and Emotion* 19 (2005): 313–332.

5 B. L. Fredrickson. "The Value of Positive Emotions," *American Scientist* 91 (2003): 330–335.

6 B. L. Fredrickson. *Positivity: Top-Notch Research Reveals the 3-1 Ration That Will Change Your Life* (New York: Random House, 2009).

7 Ibid., 16.

8 T. Amabile and S. Kramer. *The Progress Principle*.

9 Ibid., 68.

10 J. M. Smyth. "Written Emotional Expression, Effect Sizes, Outcome Types, and Moderating Variables," *Journal of Consulting and Clinical Psychology* 66 (1998): 174–184.

CHAPTER 2: FAIL FAST, FAIL OFTEN

1 Michael Bloomberg and M. Winkler. *Bloomberg by Bloomberg* (New York: John Wiley & Sons, 2001), 52.

2 David Bayles and Ted Orland. *Art & Fear: Observations on the Perils (and Rewards) of Artmaking* (Eugene, OR: Image Continuum Press, 2001).

3 Peter Sims. *Little Bets: How Breakthrough Ideas Emerge from Small Discoveries* (New York: Free Press, 2011).

4 Anne Lamott. *Bird by Bird: Some Instructions on Writing and Life* (New York: Pantheon Books, 1994).

5 Reddit. "Ask Me Anything (AMA)," 5/14/12: www.reddit.com/r/IAmA/comments/
tmlnp/louis_ck_reddit.

6 Carol Dweck. "Caution—Praise Can Be Dangerous." In *Educational Psychology in Context: Readings for Future Teachers*, Alan S. Canestrari and Bruce A. Marlowe (eds.), 207–210 (Thousand Oaks, CA: Sage Publications, 2006).

7 Ibid., 210.

8 Carol Dweck. *Mind Set: The New Psychology of Success* (New York: Random House, 2006).

CHAPTER 3: BE CURIOUS

1 Gary Wolf. "Steve Jobs: The Next Insanely Great Thing," *Wired* (February 1996).

2 Bill Strickland and Vince Rause. *Make the Impossible Possible: One Man's Crusade to Inspire Others to Dream Bigger and Achieve the Extraordinary* (New York: Crown Business, 2009).

CHAPTER 4: DON'T MARRY A JOB BEFORE YOUR FIRST DATE

1 Steve Blank. "The Lean LanchPad Class Online," http://steveblank.com/2012/08/24/the-lean-launchpad-class-online/. August 24, 2012.

2 Eric Ries. *The Lean Startup: How Today's Entrepreneurs Use Continuous Innovation to Create Radically Successful Businesses* (New York: Crown Business, 2011).

3 Potbelly Sandwich Works, LLC. Corporate Web site, "Our Story." http://www.potbelly.com/Company/OurStory.aspx.

4 Anna Quindlen. Commencement Speech, Mount Holyoke College; May 23, 1999. http://www.mtholyoke.edu/news/stories/5683096.

CHAPTER 5: THINK BIG, ACT SMALL

1 Stuart Wolpert. "Dieting Does Not Work, UCLA Researchers Report," UCLA Newsroom. April 3, 2007.

2 Robert Sutton. *Good Boss, Bad Boss* (New York: Hachette, 2010).

3 T. Amabile and S. Kramer. *The Progress Principle*.

4 Lisa D. Ordóñez, Maurice E. Schweitzer, Adam D. Galinsky, and Max H. Bazerman. "Goals Gone Wild: The Systematic Side Effects of Over-Prescribing Goal Setting," Harvard Business School Working Papers. February 11, 2009.

5 Karl Weick. "Small Wins: Redefining the Scale of Social Problems," *American Psychologist* 39(1) (1984): 40–49.

6 Peter Sims. *Little Bets: How Breakthrough Ideas Emerge from Small Discoveries* (New York: Free Press, 2011).

7 Marla "the FlyLady" Cilley. http://www.flylady.net.

8 Saras Sarasvathy. "What Makes Entrepreneurs Entrepreneurial?" (Charlottesville, VA: Darden Business Publishing, 2001). Available at Society for Effectual Action: http://www.effectuation.org/sites/default/files/research_papers/what-makes-entrepreneurs-entrepreneurial-sarasvathy_0.pdf.

CHAPTER 6: BE AN INNOVATOR

1 Jeff Dyer, Hal Gregersen, and Clayton Christensen. *The Innovator's DNA: Mastering the Five Skills of Disruptive Innovators* (Cambridge, MA: Harvard Business Review Press, 2011).

2 Ibid., 28.

3 Ibid., 102.

4 Todd Henry. *The Accidental Creative: How to Be Brilliant at a Moment's Notice* (New York: Penguin Group, 2011).

CHAPTER 7: OVERCOME ANALYSIS PARALYSIS

1 Barry Schwartz. *The Paradox of Choice: Why More Is Less* (New York: Harper Perennial, 2004).

2 D. A. Redelmeier and E. Shafir. "Medical Decision Making in Situations That Offer Multiple Alternatives," *Journal of the American Medical Association* (Jan. 25, 1992) 273 (4): 302-5.

3 Anthony Bastardi and Eldar Shafir. "On the Pursuit and Misuse of Useless Information," *Journal of Personality and Social Psychology* 75 (1) (1998): 19–32.

4 Kathleen D. Vohs, Roy F. Baumeister, Brandon J. Schmeichel, Jean M. Twenge, Noelle M. Nelson, and Dianne M. Tice. "Making Choices Impairs Subsequent Self-Control," *Journal of Personality and Social Psychology* 94 (5) (2008): 883–898.

5 Roy Baumeister, Ellen Bratslavsky, Cartrin Finkenauer, and Kathleen D. Vohs. "Bad Is Stronger Than Good," *Review of General Psychology* 5 (323) (2001): 373; Tiffany A. Ito, Jeff T. Larsen, N. Kyle Smith, and John T. Cacioppo. "Negative Information Weighs More Heavily on the Brain: The Negativity Bias in Evaluative Categorizations," *Journal of Personality and Social Psychology* 75 (4) (1998): 887–900.

CHAPTER 8: STOP RESISTING AND START LIVING

1 Steven Pressfield. *The War of Art—Break Through the Blocks and Win Your Inner Creative Battles* (New York: Warner Books, 2003).

2 Ibid., i.

3 Ibid., 8.

4 Ibid., 9.

5 John Bargh, Mark Chen, and Laura Burrows. "Automaticity of Social Behavior: Direct Effects of Trait Construct and Stereotype Activation on Action," *Journal of Personality and Social Psychology* 71 (2) (1996): 230–244.

6 Angela L. Duckworth, Christopher Peterson, Michael D. Matthews, and Dennis R. Kelly. "Grit: Perseverance and Passion for Long-Term Goals," *Journal of Personality and Social Psychology* 92 (6) (2007): 1087–1101.

7 Benjamin Bloom. *Developing Talent in Young People* (New York: Ballantine Books, 1985).

8 John J. Ratey and Eric Hagerman. *Spark: The Revolutionary New Science of Exercise and the Brain* (New York: Little, Brown and Company, 2008), 188.

9 Neil Fiore. *The Now Habit: A Strategic Program for Overcoming Procrastination and Enjoying Guilt-Free Play* (New York: Tarcher, 2007).

CHAPTER 9: IT TAKES A COMMUNITY

1 Reid Hoffman and Ben Casnocha. *The Start-up of You: Adapt to the Future, Invest in Yourself, and Transform Your Career* (New York: Crown Business, 2012).
2 Solomon Asch. "Effects of Group Pressure upon the Modification and Distortion of Judgement." In *Groups, Leadership and Men,* H. Guetzkow (ed.) (Pittsburgh, PA: Carnegie Press, 1951).
3 S. E. Asch. "Opinions and Social Pressure," *Scientific American 193* (1955): 31–35.
4 Nicholas A. Christakis and James H. Fowler. "The Spread of Obesity in a Large Social Network over 32 Years," *New England Journal of Medicine* 357 (2007): 370–379.
5 Nicholas A. Christakis and James Fowler. *Connected: The Surprising Power of Our Social Networks and How They Shape Our Lives* (New York: Little, Brown, and Company, 2009).
6 Jeff Dyer, Hal Gregersen, and Clayton M. Chrisensen. *The Innovator's DNA,* 116.
7 Ibid.
8 Ibid., 291.
9 Ron Burt. "Structural Holes and Good Ideas," *American Journal of Sociology* 110 (2) (September 2004): 349–399.
10 American Philosophical Society. History of the American Philosophical Society and the Junto. http://www.ushistory.org/franklin/philadelphia/aps.htm.

Index

If you enjoyed this book, visit

www.tarcherbooks.com

and sign up for Tarcher's e-newsletter to receive special offers, giveaway promotions, and information on hot upcoming releases.

TARCHER
PENGUIN

Great Lives Begin with Great Ideas

Connect with the Tarcher Community

• • •

Stay in touch with favorite authors!
Enter weekly contests!
Read exclusive excerpts!
Voice your opinions!

Follow us

 Tarcher Books

 @TarcherBooks

If you would like to place a bulk order of this book, call 1-800-847-5515.